Prayers and for Daily Living

By

Rob Russell

Psalm 121: 1 – 2 Good News Translation (GNT)

"¹ I look to the mountains; where will my help come from? ² My help will come from the LORD, who made heaven and earth."

Index of Prayers

Prayers/Reflections

Prayers for Daily Life

Prayers for Christian Festivals

1. An Advent prayer
2. An Advent prayer: Beginning the journey
3. A prayer for journeying through Advent
4. A prayer for others in the season of Advent
5. A Christmas prayer
6. A Christmas prayer: It's a sad time for me, Lord
7. A Christmas prayer: Help me to focus on you, Lord
8. A prayer for Christmas Day
9. A prayer for Pentecost
10. A prayer for harvest
11. A church anniversary prayer

1. A prayer/reflection

I have received bad news

Starting this conversation seems more difficult than usual.
You know, Lord, the news that I have had, and you know how I felt about it.
You know it was upsetting for both of us.
On the outside, I am trying to make light of it.
On the inside, I am a bit concerned.
Perhaps even more than a bit, if I were honest with myself.

I have many questions I want to ask.
I have so many different feelings inside me.
My heart and my mind feel confused.
At times I feel angry that this has happened,
And I want clarity and structure and a clear plan to be healthy.
At other times I just feel emotional
And I cannot put into words what I am thinking or feeling,
And that increases my frustration.

I feel a bit frightened about the future.
I feel a bit concerned about what changes will occur and how I will cope.
Perhaps most of all, I worry about how people will see me,
And if they will treat me differently.

As I speak with you today, Lord,
I know that I need to have this conversation with you.

1

I need to feel your presence.
I need you to surround my family and me
With your love, with your grace, and with your calm,
soothing balm.
I need you to increase my emotional and physical
strength in ways that only you can.
I need you to help me to keep as many of the
character traits you have given me,
So that, with your help and with the help of the
people around me,
I will remain the same person you have helped me to
become.

I give you thanks, Lord, for giving me
A caring, dedicated, committed, kind-hearted, and
loving family,
Who I know will be my rock, my strength, and my
comfort.

I thank you, Lord, for the supportive network of
friends that you have given me.
People who I know will be uplifting me in prayer
And will care for me and be there for me without
treating me any differently.

There will be days of frustration ahead of me.
There will be days when I cannot do what I used to
do,
Or cannot remember words or events that were so
familiar to me.
If these situations occur, Lord, help me to stay calm.
Help me to be kind on myself and not get frustrated.
Prompt me and remind me that in the good days and
the bad days,

I can always talk openly to my family, to my friends, and to you.
I know, Lord, that you will walk alongside me and all my family
Every minute and every hour of every day.
And it is in the sure and certain knowledge of your presence,
That I commit and dedicate my life to you, this day and always,
Amen.

2. A prayer/reflection

Caring for someone

It is so hard, Lord.
I know my beloved is the same person.
But so much has changed for both of us.
My beloved cannot remember some of the precious
moments we shared together.
They cannot remember that friends and family have
passed away.
They become frightened and confused by people
they have known for years.
Familiar places feel like hostile surroundings.
Important dates can often be forgotten,
And the name of friends cannot be recalled.

Tasks that they have enjoyed and undertaken
hundreds of times
Are now stressful and confusing activities.
What is especially difficult is that sometimes they
don't even remember who I am.
Sometimes they cannot remember my name,
Despite our spending a lifetime together.
We have shared so much, the good and the bad of
life.
We have laughed, we have joked, we have cried,
and we have talked.
But now we can't do those simple things the way we
used to.

I see the confusion in my beloved's eyes.
Sometimes they don't know why what they have said
is wrong,

4

Or why what they have done is not right.
Everything to them is normal,
But my reactions show it is not.
I feel their frustration, their fear, their uncertainty.
It hurts if I have to correct them.
I feel sad if I have to undo what they have done.
So much effort is required just for day-to-day living,
That it can be very emotionally and physically
exhausting.

Sometimes I am not as patient as I should be,
And that makes me feel horrible.
It's not my beloved's fault.
I know that outwardly, and inwardly, they are the
same person.
And my love will never end for my beloved.
But sometimes life can be very demanding.

Lord, help me in this time of change.
Give me patience when at times I feel mine is
running out.
Give me compassion when I feel frustrated.
Help me to stay calm when I want to scream and
shout at the world.
Help me to seek and accept help,
And to not see the support as a sign of weakness.
Above all, Lord, let my beloved know I love them,
And I will always love them.
For they are the other half of me,
And that will never change,
Amen.

3. A prayer/reflection

Hope in the darkness

Lord, the darkness is surrounding me
And it is consuming all the light of hope and joy that I
once had in my life.
My health, both physical and mental, is not as good
as it used to be.
My family are not around me or in contact with me as
much as they once were.
My circle of friends has diminished, and I am more
often on my own these days.
My work is not as secure as it once was,
And my job is not as enjoyable as it has been in the
past.
Life is not working out as I want it to, or how I
expected life to go.
I feel lost, confused, hopeless, and empty.
All I can see and feel is the darkness of despair.

I suppose I feel how your disciples and your
followers
Must have felt on the day after the crucifixion.
You were seen as the Messiah, sent to change
everything.
The leader who would overthrow the rule of the
Romans and set people free.
There was so much expectation placed on your
shoulders.
But on that day when you died, and the darkness
covered the earth,
The optimism and hope that your coming had
brought disappeared,

And fear and despair took over.

No one really knew why you had come to live among us.
No one could understand the divine grace of God
that beat in your heart
Until the day of the resurrection.
For on that day, the darkness realised it could not hold you.
A candle was lit. A torch was ignited. A beacon was set aglow.
The hope that would forever consume all the darkness of the world came back to life.

As I read, and reflect, on the words of Scripture,
I am reminded of the promise that you made to never leave me.
I am reminded that you will always be with those
Who dedicate their hearts and minds to you.
You are the constant source of light and hope that I need.
But I have lost my way,
And your light is not as bright as it once was in my life.

Help me, Lord, to feel your presence and to hear your voice.
I need your courage, your wisdom, your confidence, and your love.
Give me the strength to ask for help and to look for new opportunities to grow.
Help me to reach out and take hold of the support that I need.

Help me to trust the feelings you place in me about the people I meet.
Help me to know in my heart and mind how I can be free from the darkness.
Help me to always remember that your light continually burns brightly for me,
And that you will always be with me
In every decision I make, in every step I take, and in every moment I experience.
With you beside me, I know the darkness can never destroy the hope of life,
Or the plans that you have for me.
It is in your constant living and loving presence that I trust this day and always,
Amen.

4. A prayer/reflection

Showing kindness and caring for others

Lord, you call me to offer kindness far beyond what I
often feel comfortable doing.
You ask me to show the love that you have for me in
all aspects of my life.
You challenge me to offer help in situations I may not
feel comfortable being in.
To show compassion, to show understanding,
And to show practical and emotional support, where
and when I can,
Whatever a person's background, ethnicity, race,
creed, or colour.

But, Lord, it is not always easy to find the words to
help.
It is not always easy to know what I can do that will
make a difference.
I worry that I will say the wrong word.
I worry that I will do the wrong thing.
I worry that I will make a situation worse.
Perhaps most of all, Lord,
I worry about how the people I try to help will
respond to me.
I am nervous and scared about putting myself into
unfamiliar surroundings.
I worry that I will not be able to do what is required to
bring the help that is needed.

As I reflect on my fears and my uncertainties,
I am reminded of the one thing I am not doing.
I am not placing my trust in you.

When you called the disciples and sent them out
To bring your teachings to the whole world, you gave
them the Holy Spirit,
Who would be their source of wisdom, strength,
courage, and confidence.
Through trusting in you, they would always find the
right words to say.
They would always know what the right course of
action would be to take.
They would always have you
As their teacher, their companion, their guide, and
their friend.

Help me, Lord, when I feel I am being asked to give
something of myself to others,
To find the courage and the confidence to step out of
my safe space.
Help me to show kindness to other people, whatever
station in life they are at.
Help me to persevere in situations and to trust in
you,
Even when I feel my words and actions do not make
a difference.
Help me to have the wisdom to offer words and
support that can make a difference
And not be empty phrases and meaningless actions.
Help me to be generous with my time, with my
support, and with my prayers,
So that I can show others the love you have for each
and every one of us.
Guide me and keep me continually learning how I
can make a difference
In the situations you have called me to be in.
May all of us who have been called by you

Work together to harmonise and transform your world,
So that the light of hope will burn brightly and consume all the darkness,
This day and always,
Amen.

5. A prayer/reflection

Help me, Lord, my health is failing

Lord, I want to do so much more than I can at
present.
I have so many plans for places I want to go.
There are so many adventures I want to have.
I want to experience the sounds, the tastes, and the
smells
Of so many different cultures around the world.
Yet I fear I will miss out on all these experiences
because my health is deteriorating.

The medical people have told me that they can do no
more for me.
That news scared me and upset me.
I feel frustrated, Lord,
I feel downhearted, depressed, annoyed, fed up,
and, yes, a bit frightened.
I want to shout at the world and at you for letting this
happen to me.
In the cloud of pain, tiredness, and health problems
that I am experiencing,
I want to ask why this has happened to me.
I want this cup of suffering to be taken away from
me.
I want life to return to normal, to go back to the way it
was a few months ago.
Yet I sense that is not your plan for me, not yet,
anyway, and maybe not ever.

You have given me a new station in life.
I have a new reality to cope with and I don't know
how long I will be here.
I don't know if I will get better and move back closer
to my old life,
Or if my health will continue to fail
And I will move closer to being with you in your
eternal kingdom.

In my pain, anger, and frustration of this uncertainty,
I cannot hear your voice.
But I know that you are with me and you are trying to
help me.
As I express my feelings to you, Lord, and as I
confess my thoughts and fears,
I need to accept your presence into my heart, into
my mind, and into my body.
I need to feel your peace flowing through me, and I
need you to help me
To find a calmness and strength to cope with this
new reality.

Whatever you have planned for me in the days and
weeks that are ahead,
Help me to have the courage to manage these
experiences.
Help me to have the strength to ask for help,
When I cannot do the tasks I have always been able
to complete.
Help me to be gracious, help me to be
understanding,
And help me to continue to love you and the people
around me.

I am surrounded by so much love and by the prayers
of so many people.
Help me to accept that love,
And to embrace the prayerful support that is being
given to me.
Most of all, Lord, don't leave me,
Even when, at times, I may not always appreciate
your presence.
Guide me, Lord, and be the rod and staff that
comfort me.
Be the light of eternal life that leads me on this
journey.
Be the source of comfort, love, and reassurance to
me and to my family
In all that we experience.
Be my friend, Lord, and nurture, guard, and protect
me this day and always,
Amen.

6. A reflection

Lord, you are standing in front of me

You are standing in front of me, Lord,
And I can't look at you.
I bow my head in honour and in awe of your
presence.
My heart is racing.
My knees are knocking.
I feel both excited and nervous at the same time.
I feel you looking at me,
But I cannot look at you.
I cannot raise my head.
I am not worthy of having you visit me.
I am not worthy of being in your presence.
I feel ashamed,
Because I know I have not been the person you told
me to be.
I know I have let you down.
I know you will tell me how bad I have been.
I know you will judge me.
You will judge both my words and my actions.
I want to hide from you.

But something inside me is telling me to look up.
Whether I want to or not, I feel drawn to you.
My head moves upwards, as does my whole body.
There is an overwhelming feeling in me that I must
look at you.
My face has to meet your face.
My eyes have to meet your eyes.

As your face comes into my field of vision,

I first see your lips.
They are speaking words of encouragement to me.
So I move more quickly so that I can see you more clearly.
Then I see your eyes.
They are full of love and compassion for me.
As I meet your gaze,
I feel a calming presence come over me.
I feel a peace that flows through my body from head to toe.
I have never felt like this before,
I don't have any cares, any worries, or any health problems.
You are drawing all of them out of me.
I feel confident, and I must speak to you.
I must tell you how much you mean to me.
I must thank you for all you have done for me.
I am not the person I am for me, but for you, Lord.
You have given me so much,
And you have helped me to do so many things
That I would have never thought possible.
You have held my hand each day.
In really difficult times,
You have carried me and given me courage.
You have been with me at all times.
And yet,
While my heart wants to say all these things,
I just look at you, without saying anything.
I am smiling at you, Lord,
Just as you are smiling at me.
And I have this feeling
That you know all the words I want to say.
You know all the things I feel ashamed of and want your forgiveness for.

You know all the things I am grateful for.
You know all the things I feel blessed to have.

As I look at you, Lord,
I feel accepted, understood, cared for, forgiven,
encouraged, and loved.
I feel the words 'Thank you,' on my lips.
As I speak the words to you,
I feel your grace passing over me.
I feel my bond with you strengthened,
My belief in you deepened,
My courage and faith in you enhanced,
And our loving relationship refreshed.
I feel ready, Lord, ready to go on,
Ready to walk the journey with you.
Ready to face the days, weeks, and years
You have planned for me.

For I know, Lord,
That we will walk through these days together.
And that you will always be with me,
Smiling at me,
Speaking words of encouragement to me,
Forgiving me, and guiding me.
Thank you, Lord, thank you.
Amen.

7. A prayer/reflection

Talking with God

Talking to you, Lord, should be easy. After all, you
have known me all my life.
Even when I was not always aware of your presence
around me,
I know that you were always beside me.
At times I just did not notice your presence
Or maybe I chose not to acknowledge you were
there next to me.
But as I have grown and as I have progressed,
I have come to realise the importance of speaking
with you.

Talking to you can help me to make my thoughts
clearer.
It can help me to get a better understanding of
The day-to-day situations that I experience.
It can help me to try and stay calm
When I may otherwise become lost to any anger or
frustration that is inside me.

Yet there are days, maybe too many days, when I
find it hard to speak to you.
I find it hard to express to you what is in my heart
and on my mind.
I find it hard to put into words the emotions I am
feeling.

It should be easy to speak to you.
I know what I need to do: sit quietly and speak
openly.

Yet that does not always work.
Sometimes in my mind, Lord, I have too much going on.
I have so many emotions inside me
That I cannot sort through them and express them to you.
I know that if I ask, Lord, you will help me.
But too often, Lord, I give up or don't try and put into words
The events of my life that are causing me the most concern and stress.

Lord, you experience everything that happens in my life
In exactly the same way I do.
You share with me the ups and downs on my journey.
You hear every word I speak.
You feel every emotion that moves through my heart and in my soul.
You see every thought I have and share each moment of my daily life.
Nothing of me is hidden from you.

When I cannot express what is in my heart and in my mind,
Encourage me to be quiet in your presence
And to know that you are with me in the silence.
Help me to realise that I do not need
To phrase my thoughts and feelings in complex words and sentences.
Help me to speak with you using simple words, and help me not be concerned

If my conversation with you does not always make sense.
Help me to remember that you already know about me and where I am in life.
You know what I need and who I need to help me.
You know how I feel and you know what I think.
You are my companion, my friend, my helper, my rock, on which I can depend,
And my salvation from all the challenges that life can bring.
Help me to always feel your presence and to never forget that you are my God.
You will never leave me and you will always love and accept me,
Amen.

8. A prayer/reflection

The dawn chorus

I love this time of the day, Lord.
A time when we can be still and quiet together
And watch the world you created wake up.
I love to see the sun rise and the golden rays of light
start to penetrate the darkness.
I love the way the sunlight casts away the gloom of
the night
And heralds the start of a new and exciting day.
I love to hear the birds exercising their voices
And beginning their chorus to each other.
Waking each other up,
And encouraging each other to begin the search for
the first meal of the day.
I love the smell of the fresh morning dew on the
grass
As nature begins to shed its nightly cloak
And prepares itself for another day of growing under
your care.
Sometimes, Lord, the beginning of the day is
shrouded in grey,
And rain splatters in patterns on my windows.
Sometimes the wind roars through my ears as it
blows away the debris of the night.
But always, Lord, the beginning of the day
Is an amazing time to be in your presence.

Being awake at this time in the morning is always a
special time for me
Because it is a time for me to see and hear your
presence.

It enables me to see how you bring alive all that you created.
It enables me to see the changing colours of the plants and the flowers
As they are uncovered from their blanket of darkness.
It enables me to smell the delights of your creation.
I get to experience the fragrant offering of all your earthly gifts
Just as you intended them to be,
Without the interruption of the noise and the haste of my daily life.
It enables me to gently move into the day ahead.

Each day, Lord, the world around me changes.
New birds and other members of your wildlife family come and visit my garden.
Old friends come back to say hello and to offer me their morning greeting.
The plants and the flowers change colour and flourish.
The early morning delivery people whistle a different tune.
The world that you entrusted to me changes just a bit more
And you challenge me to see it.
It is so easy, Lord, as the day rushes in, to ignore what is around me.
It is so easy to become focused on the challenges and difficulties
That day-to-day life can cause.
It is so easy to focus on the negative parts of my life
And to concentrate my energy on all the things I feel I don't have,

And to not be thankful for the gifts you have given me.

As I prepare myself for the hours to come,
I ask you to help me to be constantly aware of
The ever-changing landscape around me.
Help me to be thankful for all that you have given to me.
Help me to embrace with love in my heart all that you have created.
Help me to be more aware and gracious of the dawn's early calling.
Help me to be a better guardian and friend of
This little part of your world that you have entrusted to me.
Help our time together in every part of the day be full of hope and joy
Because you created a wonderful world.
Speak to me, Lord, and help me to find ways that I can bring others to know
What joy it is to share together with you at the beginning of the dawn chorus,
Amen.

9. A prayer/reflection

Christmas Eve

Lord, the time of Advent is nearly over.
The time of preparation is almost done.
And the day, when I sing of your birth, is just a few
hours away.

As I prepare myself to celebrate your arrival,
I ask you to help me to calm down, both mentally
and physically.
Help me to stop, to listen, to reflect, and to be stilled
in your presence.

I hear the familiar lines of Scripture,
And I wonder how I would have responded
Had I been there that starry night.

I marvel at the strength, courage, commitment, and
dedication
That all the people had in the story of your birth.
Mary and Joseph, a young couple, not even married,
But thrust into parenthood for the first time
And given the responsibility to bring up the light of
the world.

Such love they showed to each other,
So much trust they had both in each other and in
you.
They didn't have a room booking.
They were not sure what they would find when they
got to Bethlehem.
But they travelled the long, hard miles

To reach the place of destiny, so that your journey
on earth could begin.

I think of the shepherds, a group of people who
never looked for attention,
Who were always in the shadows,
But you called them and brought them into the centre
of the story.
You sent messengers to seek them out,
To speak to them, to inspire their hearts
To do something that they would never have
dreamed of doing,
And to go on a mission to find a babe in a manger.

You gave them the courage to leave their sheep and
go into the busy town.
You gave them the confidence to approach a family
they did not know,
And offer all that they had to give,
In praise and thanks of their master, their protector,
Their guide, and their eternal friend, who would
always take care of them.

There is so much of the season of Christmas
That is wrapped up in paper and tinsel.
So much that is carried away in the celebrations,
music,
Bright lights, and Christmas puddings,
That the simplicity of what happened all those years
ago is almost lost.

As I prepare myself this night to rejoice in your
coming,
Fill my life, not with food and presents,

But with optimism and hope.

Help me to have the trust, commitment, dedication, and love
That Mary and Joseph showed when they heard your word.
Help me to have the courage, the confidence, and the mental strength,
That the shepherds had when they stepped out of their safe space.
Help me to feel the choirs of angels singing in my heart
As I remember all that you have done for me.
Help me to make the season of Advent and of Christmas about you
And to use the gifts and talents you have given to me
To introduce you to those who do not yet know you
But who are longing for you and searching for you,
Amen.

10. A prayer/reflection

New Year's Day

Lord, today is New Year's Day.
A time when I can reflect on another year that has passed,
A time to review the events of the last twelve months,
A time to reset myself to face the challenges that lie before me,
A time to renew my relationships with the people around me.
It is a time for me to make a new start in the parts of my life that I need to change.

Lord, each year brings its own special memories,
And I give thanks for your presence in each moment.
I give thanks for all that you have given to me.
Although this past year has not always been easy,
The strength and support of the people around me, and
The network of friends you have helped me to build,
Have provided me with so much comfort, strength, and joy.

I ask that you help me to show how much my friends and family mean to me,
To help me to make the most of the time I have been given,
And to make space in my life for those who I love.

As I reflect on another milestone,
Another year you have blessed me with,

I ask that you continue to help me develop,
To help me to grow, spiritually and emotionally.
Help me to become wiser and to make good choices.
I know I will make mistakes, Lord.
I know that sometimes I won't make the right
decisions.
When that happens, Lord, give me humility.
Speak to me and challenge me to acknowledge my
errors,
And to apologise when I am wrong.

I know, Lord, that there will be challenging days this
year.
There will be moments, Lord,
When I feel I do not have the strength and the
courage
To face the days ahead of me.
In those moments, Lord, help me to feel your loving
embrace.
Help me to ask for help when I cannot achieve my
goals on my own.
Help me, Lord, to recognise that,
With your help and with the loving support of the
people around me,
I can achieve anything. I can overcome any difficult
times.
I can be a better person.

Help me to become richer in my experiences and in
my understanding.
So that, as I journey along the path of life this year,
I will have even more to celebrate with you
And with my friends, family, and those I love,
Amen.

11. A prayer for Epiphany

The journey of the Three Wise Men

Lord, as I listen to the story of Christmas,
I am reminded at how subtle and yet how strong your
call can be.
You placed a star in the sky.
A star like so many others that night,
But a star that shone more brightly
And which had a special mission to perform.
It had a special journey to take.
It had a wondrous message to deliver.

I have often wondered, Lord, what was so special
about that star
Which made the wise men know they had to leave
home
And travel thousands of miles over many years
In order to follow wherever it led.
I wonder if the wise men knew they were going to
Bethlehem.
I wonder if they knew what they were seeking.
I wonder if they knew why they had the three gifts of
gold, frankincense, and myrrh.
I wonder if they were excited by the message you
sent them
Or were worried about the sacrifices they would have
to make.

Yet, Lord, the wise men did follow your star.
They had the wisdom, and they had the knowledge
To make the journey you were asking them to take.
They had the courage, the commitment,

The dedication, and the conviction, to follow where
you led.
They knew the paths they travelled would not be
easy or secure.
They probably knew it was a long road ahead of
them.
But they knew this was the adventure they had to go
on.

As I reflect on the wise men's story,
I wonder if I have the strength of character
And the commitment to make the journey the wise
men made.
I am reminded that it is not always easy to make the
journey you ask me to take.
Your call, Lord, often requires me to take a leap of
faith.
To make a commitment that could be for many
years.
To go on a journey to a destination I may not know,
To an end point that may not be clear to me.
But to a place in my life journey where I need to be.

Not always, Lord, is the road of life smooth and
clear.
Many times obstacles appear in front of me.
There are dark times and times when I find it hard
To see the star that you are asking me to follow.

Help me to always know where I should look to find
your presence.
Help me to always know you will lead me and guide
me.

Help me to always know that your light will remain in the sky for me, burning brightly,

And guiding me towards the work you want me to do, And bringing me closer to our eternal life together, Amen.

12. A prayer/reflection

Lent

Lord, the time of Lent is near,
And I thank you for this time to reflect on the
sacrifices that you have made for me.
Lent reminds me of the forty days and forty nights
When you were tested both mentally and physically
in the desert.
A time when you had to give up your way of life,
And follow the path your Father had prepared for
you.

I often hear it said that following you is never easy,
But Lent reminds me that you made sacrifices
That were far more extreme than those I am asked
to make.
You endured far more suffering than I am asked to
endure.
You were offered temptations that I cannot fully
understand.
Yet in all of this, you held true.
Your commitment did not falter, and your love
remained steadfast
In your Father and my Father, in your God and my
God.

In this season of preparation and the journey to the
cross on Good Friday,
Help me to understand more clearly what you have
done for me.
Help me to understand that Lent is much more than

Giving up chocolate, ice cream, or cakes. It is about
me making a commitment.
It is about me making a sacrifice in your name
That can make a difference to the people around me.
It is about me doing something I would not normally
do
That will show my dedication and my love for you.

I will never know why you chose to die for me.
I will never know why you made the ultimate sacrifice
to help me.
But I know I will, always and forever, be grateful that
you made that sacrifice.
I will always give you thanks
For your unconditional dedication and commitment to
me.
I will always be thankful for your love,
Which is constant, and which surrounds me each
day.
Help me in this time of Lent to give to others what
you have given to me
And to understand that in sharing your love I am
making your sacrifice worthwhile.

I may not be able to endure all that you went through
physically.
I may not feel I am able to make grand gestures that
will make a difference.
But from this station in life that you have me resting
at, speak to me and guide me.
Help me to know what more I can do.
Encourage me to spend time in quiet reflection with
you.
Inspire my thoughts.

Give me a more compassionate and understanding heart and mind.
Help me to realise that small gestures can have A big effect on those who receive them.
Make my journey through Lent, and to the cross, Be an offering and a sacrifice worthy of your teaching,
So that together on Easter Day we celebrate more than your resurrection.
We celebrate my renewed commitment to your service and to your glorious name,
Amen.

13. A prayer/reflection

Palm Sunday

Lord, as you arrived into Jerusalem that day,
They waved palm branches and threw their cloaks
on the ground.
They cheered, and exalted your name.
They shouted loud hosannas and cried blessings to
you.
They believed you were going to get rid of the old
guard
And start a new political system.
You were the leader of their revolutionary army.

But you rode a donkey, as a sign of humility,
And as a symbol that you had come into our world to
serve and not to be served.
You didn't carry weapons or use armour.
You came to teach, to educate, to heal, and to lead
the people back to your father.
When you spoke everyone listened.
You inspired all who heard you. You healed all who
cried out to you for help.

You forgive all who confess their failings and admit
their human frailties.
You accept everyone, wherever they are on their
journey of life.

You came as a humble servant and you taught us
That we should be the servants of each other.
You came to tell us of God's unconditional and
eternal love.

You came to tell us of a life beyond our human understanding.
You came to show us God's grace and mercy.
You came to set an example of how life could be if we put others before ourselves.
You came to show compassion, forgiveness, truth, and divine love,
Which was spoken through your actions and not just through your words.

Lord, on this Palm Sunday, I celebrate and wave my palm branches.
I sing hosannas to my Lord and King.
I thirst and hunger for your word to teach me and guide me.
I rejoice at your presence in my life and in the hope that springs eternal each day Because I have you as my guiding light.
I ask for your blessings to be poured into my daily life.

Yet on that day when you travelled into Jerusalem,
You knew what was in the hearts and minds of the people who exalted you.
You knew far better than any of your followers
The betrayal and the lies that you would have to endure.
You knew about the denials that were to come, even from your closest friends.
You knew about the pain and suffering you would have to go through.
You knew our human weaknesses and our abilities to be cruel to each other.
Yet you still love all the people in this world.

You give us all the chance of redemption.

As I journey to the cross with you,
Give me the strength, wisdom, courage, and
confidence
To walk the path you have asked me to take
And to carry the cross you have asked me to bear.
I ask that you speak to me and challenge my
thoughts and perceptions.
I ask that you help me to show through my actions
your divine love and compassion.
I ask that you help me to be kind to myself and to
others.
I ask that you strengthen my weaknesses and admit
my failings
So that I can be drawn more closely to you.

Help me to always keep the light of your eternal
presence burning brightly in my life, So that others
will see your love reflected in my words and actions.
Help me to make all that I do each day be an offering
worthy of
Your love, your guidance, and your teachings,
Which shape my life this day and always,
Amen.

14. A prayer/reflection

Good Friday

Lord, each year I reflect on this day,
And wonder why it is called 'Good Friday'.
I cannot see what is good about this day.
It seems such a contrast to how I feel.

When I think about what happened to you,
I shudder at the suffering you went through.
You came into our world to be the light of our
heavenly father.
A light that brought hope, understanding, grace, and
love.
You brought healing and kindness.
And the world rejected you.
You were spat at.
You were jeered.
You were mocked.
You were whipped.

Your beautiful hands that had blessed children,
Hands that had been placed on the ears of the deaf
so that they could hear,
Hands that had been placed on the eyes of the blind
so that they could see,
Were pierced with rusty nails and pinned to a cross.
Your feet that had walked around the country,
Bringing a message of salvation and peace,
Were nailed to a cross, and you were lifted high
So that all around could see you.

And then you died.

And at that moment, the hope of the world died with you.
The darkness blocked out the light.

You died ... for me, even though you have done so much in my life.
You went so much further than I could have expected.
You died for me because you care so much about me.
In your death, you took away my sins.
You told me that if I truly repent and say I am sorry,
You will forgive me, and I will be born anew,
Given another chance.
A chance to be a better person,
To be a caring, understanding, and loving person.
You gave me a chance so that I can try and be a little like you
In how I am with the people around me.

Lord, forgive me when I am sometimes blind to your love.
Forgive me when my words and actions do not always show
The love you have for me.
Forgive me when I do not always respond to you as you would want me to.
Help me, Lord, to love the people around me as you love me.
Help me to make your sacrifice worthwhile.
Help me to show what you mean to me,
And how much you love me
In everything I do and say,
Amen.

15. A prayer/reflection

Good Friday

The sacrifice, Lord, you made for me

Lord, as I prepare myself for today,
The day when I remember what was done to you,
My heart aches and your pain and suffering
dominate my thoughts.
I shudder when I remember the brutality of what was
done to you.
The jeers, the taunts, the cuts, the scars, the nails.
The cross that you were made to carry.
A cross that you were nailed to and lifted up on,
Because people were afraid of you and what your
presence could mean.

You endured so much pain and suffering.
You accepted all that had been planned for you.
You followed your Father's wishes, with humility and
with love in your heart.
In your pain and anguish,
You allowed yourself to be nailed to a cross and
lifted high,
So that the world would understand who and what
you are.
And you did all that because you love me.

You are the Son of God.
The counsellor who listens to all.
The parent and guardian who nurtures and guides.

The still, calm, and peaceful presence that provides
rest and reassurance.
But that is not how people saw you.

You were adored by many, listened to by crowds of
hundreds.
And exalted with cheers, cloaks, and palm branches.

But you were feared by some,
And that fear spread and infected the hearts and
minds
Of the people you had been sent to save.
You were rejected
You were betrayed.
You were abused, insulted, and beaten.
Your friends denied that they knew you.
You were sentenced to death.
Your hands and feet were pierced with nails and
your side was pierced by a sword.
You hung on a cross in the noonday sun,
And there you took your final breath.
You died, for me.

As I reflect on this day, I ask you to open my eyes
and my ears.
I ask you to inspire my thoughts and to give me a
kind and understanding heart.
Take the sadness that I feel at what you went
through,
And turn it into the catalyst for optimism that you
intended your crucifixion to be.
Take my guilt at having done so many things
differently
From the way you wanted me to,

And turn it into the beacon of light and hope that you want me to be in your world.
Take the love I have for you, and make it shine in all the dark places of my world.

Every day I am grateful for the ultimate sacrifice that you made for me.
Every day I am grateful that you have helped me to see
That I can have an eternal life with you.
Through your death you gave me a chance to be forgiven for my mistakes.
Through your pain and suffering you showed me
That you will never leave me and you will always forgive me.
You encourage me in every moment of every day to acknowledge my failings,
To confess, and to truly repent all that I have done wrong.
You reassure me that if I do all these things, you will help me to find a better life.

Through my prayers, my thoughts, my words, and my actions,
Help me, Lord, this day, to make my life more fulfilling.
Help me to make better decisions
And to be more loving, compassionate, and understanding.
Help my life and everything I say and do
Be more beneficial to the people around me.
Help me to reflect the significance of your sacrifice and all that you mean to me,
Through all that I do, this day and always. Amen.

16. A prayer/reflection

Easter Day

On this day, Lord, I feel so happy and elated.
I sing your praises.
I celebrate that death did not hold you.
I give praise and thanksgiving that you have risen.
I give joyful worship that you are alive.

This day is so special, Lord,
Because I thought you were gone and hope was lost
to the darkness.
But on this day, Lord, you showed me
That the light of the world cannot be conquered by
darkness.
You showed me that hope and everlasting joy and
life are found in you.
From this day I received optimism, strength,
courage, and confidence.
You reminded me that wherever I go and whatever I
experience,
You have been there before me.
You showed me that you are the light of my life,
And that you will always burn for me.
You will illuminate the path I walk as I follow you.
When I stumble and lose my way,
You will reach out to me and support me.
You will always welcome me back into your arms.

And what is really special, Lord,
Is that you do not just do this for me on Easter Day,
But you do this for me every day of my life.
And that is why I will always love you
And sing your praises. Amen

17. A prayer/reflection

Calmness and peace in a world of conflict

As I reflect on the violence in the world,
My heart aches with the pain and suffering that is
being experienced.
Wars, conflict, fighting: it all seems so senseless.
And there are too many situations where attacks and
fighting are continuing.
I cannot fully comprehend the emotional trauma that
people have gone through.
I cannot grasp the suffering they have endured.

As I spend this time thinking about conflict,
It is you, Lord, who I turn to and pray for your help.
I know, Lord, that there are people who are still
suffering this day
From the traumas they have seen and experienced
in the past.
I ask, Lord, that you be a tangible presence
In the lives of those who have been injured.
Help those who are in need to have the courage to
ask for assistance.
Help them to know that they do not make the journey
towards recovery alone.
Help them to know that they are accepted and loved
for the person they are today.

You, Lord, are the Prince of Peace.
You bring compassion and understanding into the
hearts and souls of everybody.
I ask that you provide reconciliation and peace to this
troubled world.

I ask you to help me to try and make sense of the senseless acts of other people.
Help me to know what I can do that may make a difference in this world,
Which can so often feel violent and aggressive.
Help me to have a better understanding of the emotional and physical effects
That violence and living through traumatic experiences have on the people involved.
Help me to know what I can do that will make a difference.
Help me to listen more, to speak less, and to be a calm, reassuring presence
For the people who confide in me and ask for help.

Constantly remind me to uplift, in my prayer time, those who have been
Injured, traumatised, or emotionally and physically scarred by life.
Most of all, Lord, be the beacon of love and light
In the lives of all who are traumatised.
Help us all to receive the calmness and peace that is found with you,
Amen.

18. A prayer/reflection

Buying a new house

I have decided to move house, Lord, and I have put an offer on my dream home.
Moving house feels really exciting.
I have a new place to go to and new neighbours to meet.
I have new rooms to decorate and furnish.
I have a new space to call my own.
I have a new community to explore.

But moving is also so stressful.
I worry that the offer will not be accepted.
I worry that the chain of house sales will collapse and I will not be able to move.
I worry about all the packing and all the boxes I will have to get
And fill with the memories I have created in the place where I live right now.
I worry that I will not be able to get the furniture out of this house
And into my new home.
I worry that I will not settle into my new surroundings
And that moving will not be all that I had hoped it would be.
I worry that the neighbours will not like me.
There is so much that I worry about, Lord,
That I am in danger of losing the positives that this move can provide.

As I prepare to move house, Lord, help me to stop worrying and to trust in you.
There are so many parts of this process that I cannot control or affect
And, while that is frustrating and scary,
I need to let go and have faith in where you want me to be.
Guide me, Lord, and let me know that this house move is
The right next step for me to make on my journey in life.
Help me to stay calm, Lord, and not to worry about
The stages in this move that are beyond my control.
Ease my fears, Lord, and help me to remember that
You will be with me in every part of this process.
Help me to feel your reassuring presence as I go along the journey.

I know that you are my guiding light, Lord, and if this house move is to happen,
And this new place is where you want me to be, you will help me to make it happen.
Help me to take the positive out of all the situations I experience.
Help me to have the confidence to meet the people you send into my life.
Help me to embrace this new place I am going to.
Help me to enjoy the opportunities that you give me in this place.
Help me to trust in you and to trust that you will provide me with all I need
To cope, and to manage all that will happen in the coming days, weeks, and months.

Let me store all the experiences I have in my
memory bank of life

So that I can use each moment to help me as I move
along the road of life.
May each moment of this move enrich my life and
deepen my relationship with you So that I can grow
in confidence, in wisdom, in love, and
In the sure and certain knowledge that you will
always be with me,
Amen.

19. A prayer/reflection

Time in the kitchen

As I work in my kitchen, Lord, I feel a sense of
purpose and of belonging.
This is a place I am most comfortable,
And where I can find so much joy and fulfilment.
I have spent many wonderful hours in this place,
Looking at recipes, weighing ingredients, planning
meals,
And using the gifts and talents that you have
provided me with.

I love to cook, Lord. I love to bake and I love to
produce meals and cakes
That I can share with family, with friends, and with
people who I may never meet.
Providing food, Lord, is one of my ways to show
The love and commitment I have for you.

Not all my baking and cooking goes the way I
planned.
Sometimes I can get frustrated with my ingredients,
with the equipment I use,
And maybe at times with myself.
But mostly, Lord, in this place, as I whisk and stir, I
feel a connection with you.
I feel your presence moving around and within me,
inspiring me and guiding me.

Thank you, Lord, for giving me the gifts that you have provided me with.

Continue to be my guiding light as I prepare my ingredients

And lovingly produce the meals and cakes.

If my cooking or baking does not go according to plan, help me to stay calm.

Help me to be gentle on myself and to use the gifts you have given me to be creative

And to find solutions to turn what I would call near disaster into triumph.

Help me to continue to pour my heart and soul into my cooking

And to reflect the love I have for you in the food I produce.

Help me to continue learning and to look for new ways I can develop my skills.

Help me to be imaginative, and to never be afraid to try and make something new.

Help me to always remember that you will be with me in everything I try

And that you will help me to make a success of whatever I attempt.

The day may come, Lord, when I cannot do as much in the kitchen

As I have in the past.

If that day comes, Lord, and I find baking and cooking physically demanding,

Encourage me not to give up.

Encourage me to pace my time in the kitchen,

And to ask for help as and when I need it.

Help me to look for new ways in which I can enjoy and share my passion.

Help me to be a good teacher as well as a good listener,
So that I can pass on my talents and skills to others.

I have so much to be grateful for, and I thank you
That you have provided me with the opportunities to share my gifts with others.
You, Lord, are the bread of life, and I thank you that you have helped me to feed
So many people through the food you have helped me to prepare.
Help me to continue enjoying what I do and to enjoy our time together.
Let everything I do in the kitchen be an offering that is worthy of your teaching
And of our continued commitment to each other,
Amen.

20. A prayer/reflection

Time in the garden

Lord, spending time in my garden is such a special
moment of the day.
I feel your calm and soothing presence
As I go about the flower beds and the vegetable
patches.
I feel a connection with you, and a sense of purpose,
Whenever I come out to work in our garden together.

When I am out amid the soil and my fingers are in
the earth,
My senses come alive to the beauty of your world.
As I pot plants and seedlings,
I feel the optimism and joy at helping nature to grow.
When I have my trowel in hand I feel your presence
Guiding me and encouraging me.
You speak to me and help me know where I should
place
Each vegetable, each fruit, each flower, each bush,
and each tree.
You help me to know where the best place is in my
garden
So that everything we plant together will have the
best chance to receive
The light, the shade, and the water that you provide
to help it all grow and flourish.

As I plant my carrots, lettuce, potatoes, strawberries,
and blackcurrants,
As I pot up my dwarf beans and sweet peas,

As I tend my rose bushes and tie back my
sunflowers,
As I carefully look over the garden for weeds,
I feel a sense of purpose and a sense of belonging.
I feel the responsibility that you have given me
To look after this bounteous array of your earthly
gifts.
I feel our relationship deepen and our bond grow,
As I play my part in tending for this small corner of
your world.

Thank you, Lord, for giving me the opportunity to
work in this wonderful garden.
Thank you for giving me the skills and knowledge to
take seeds
And help them to grow into the beautiful creations
that you had planned them to be.

The day may come, Lord, when I cannot do as much
in the garden as I want to do.
If that day comes, Lord, encourage me to seek help
when I need it
And to look for new ways in which I can enjoy and
share this passion.

I have so much to be grateful for and I thank you for
guiding my life with you,
And for giving me such an abundant harvest, which I
can look upon each day.
You, Lord, are the gardener of life, and I thank you
that you have helped me
To plant a world full of colour and nutrition with the
flowers, fruit, and vegetables
That decorate the landscape that is before me.

As I look upon this garden you have helped me to create,
I feel joy and happiness at what we have achieved together.
Help me to continue enjoying what I do and to enjoy our time together.
Let everything I do in the garden be an offering
That is worthy of your nurturing and caring ways,
And let it be a reflection of our continued commitment to each other,
Amen.

21. A prayer/reflection

Swimming in the pool

Thank you, Lord, for the time when I can go swimming.
For the time I spend in the pool, relaxing with friends and exercising my body.
Being in the water, Lord, and swimming up and down,
Calms me and helps me to relax all my muscles.
It can ease the pain in my joints and helps me to move a little more easily.
It gives me the chance to clear my mind and let the worries of the day float away, Even if only for a short time.
It allows the whole of me to receive that extra support that I need
When I let the power of the ripples in the water take the strain.

Sometimes I need to hold the hand of a friend or loved one
To help me to move around the pool.
Sometimes I need the tangible support and encouragement
To help me to go further into the water and maybe even go deeper into the pool.
Sometimes I need the courage and the confidence to let go
And venture out into the water on my own,
To swim my own strokes, however graceful or ungraceful they may seem.

Sometimes I can just walk close to the side of the pool,
Knowing I can hold on to the rail if I feel I need the support.
But always, Lord, I know that my friends and the people in the pool
Are there to help me if I get into difficulties.

Spending time in the pool reminds me of my life with you.
You support me, Lord, in the same way as the water helps me.
Just like the pool, when I look for you in my life,
You surround me with your vast and never-ending love.
You help my body to move even though it may be in pain and feel overburdened.
You provide the buoyancy I need that helps me to stay afloat
Even when at times I feel like I may drown.
You help my mind to unwind and give me the chance to reset
And to take a fresh look at the situations in my life.
You encourage me to go out on my own and to grow and develop
So that I can improve my talents and the abilities you have given me to help others.

Thank you, Lord, that, when spending time swimming, I feel so connected with you.
Thank you that, in this time with family and friends,
I feel the support that you have provided me with.
Thank you for having given me this chance

To help me to improve my physical and mental well-being.

Thank you for having given me the chance to meet new people, and
To develop new friendships as we enjoy the shared experience of floating together.
Encourage me, Lord, to keep going into the pool,
Even when there are days when I feel I cannot make the time.
Help me to remember that spending time in the pool
Is so much more than just swimming in the water.
It is another chance for me to feel your love and support.
It is a chance for me to feel the energy that inspires me to be the servant
That you have called me to be this day and always,
Amen.

Prayers for daily life

1. The gift of a child

Lord, I feel so happy that I am going to have a baby,
To have a child to look after, teach, help, and grow.
It is such a wonderful gift.
But I know the gift comes with responsibilities.
Help me, Lord, to be a good parent.
Help me to be a good example.
To get the balance right between discipline and
nurture.
Help me to be an encouraging parent.
And help me to be a calm and understanding parent.
Help me let my child grow as you have planned for
them.
And help me to be a good teacher of your ways,
Through my words and my actions,
Amen.

2. Baptism prayer

Lord, as I prepare for my child to be baptised,
I ask that you welcome them into your family.
Place into their heart your eternal fire,
So that it will burn within them as a source of
calmness and hope.
Guide my child and help them to be open to your
word.
Teach my child and help them to learn your ways.
Inspire my child and help them always to follow their
dreams.
Lead my child, so that whatever path they follow,
Your light will be there to show them the way.
Love my child, so that they will feel your comfort and
peace.
Bless my child, and fill them with your holy presence.
Always be near my child, Lord, and keep them safe.
Help them to know and feel the love you have for
each one of us.
And help me, Lord, to show how much my child
means to me,
Through my words and my actions, this day and
always,
Amen.

3. A prayer for parents

Being a parent, Lord, feels a privilege and an honour.
But it feels daunting and, at times, overwhelming.
I want to do the best for my child.
I want them to have every chance and opportunity to fulfil your plan for them.
But I am scared that I am not up to the task.
I am scared that I will do something wrong.
I worry that my child will do things that will upset me and annoy me.
How will I react? How can I be supportive?

Lord, when life does not go according to plan,
Help me to remember to turn to you.
Remind me to look and listen for you.
Give me wisdom and help me to find the words
That will offer constructive advice and reassurance.
Keep me calm and help me not to overreact to unexpected situations.
Help me to remember that making mistakes,
And doing things differently from the way I would do them,
Are ways of learning and growing.

But above all, Lord, keep my child safe and never leave them.
Even if they leave you, Lord, always remain close to them,
And also help them to know that no matter what they do,
I will always love them, just as you have always loved me. Amen.

4. First day at school

Lord, today is the first day I will let my child go.
It is the first time I will not have my child with me all day.
They are continuing their journey of education,
But it is a new setting, a new place,
And I will not be with them to help them.
I feel nervous and apprehensive.
I know this is a natural part of growing up,
But I worry that they will not make friends.
I worry that my child will be bullied. I worry that they will feel lonely.

Be with my child, Lord, as they go into this new place.
Bless their friendships, their playtime, and their learning.
Help them to know what to say and do in new situations.
If they feel lonely, surround them with your loving presence.
If they are bullied, help them to be strong and to ask for help.
Help them to stay calm in difficult times.
Give them courage and wisdom.
Help them to enjoy this new experience.
But most of all, Lord, help them to remember
How much I love them and care for them, in all the situations they go through,
Amen.

5. A prayer for undertaking examinations

Lord, I feel nervous about this examination.
I have revised, but so much of my future depends on the outcome of this test.
I feel so nervous I can hardly speak.
I worry that my mind will go blank in the exam.
I worry that I won't understand what the questions ask me to do.
I worry that I won't be able to remember the information I need to write the answers.
I am anxious that the people around me will go through the paper
So much quicker and better than me.
Above all, Lord, I worry that I will fail.
And I will let myself and my family down.

Lord, be with me during this exam.
Keep me calm.
If I am not sure what the question asks me to do,
Remind me to reread the question.
Help me to pause and to not panic if I become stuck.
Give me wisdom, Lord, so that I will remember what I have learnt.
Give me confidence so that I can work through each question
With boldness and assurance.
Let me feel your loving, guiding, and inspirational presence as I do this exam.
But most of all, Lord,
Encourage me to be kind to myself and to trust in you this day and always,
Amen.

6. A prayer for beginning study at university

The time has come, Lord, for me to start my
university studies.
A time when I will progress in my education and
embrace studying at a higher level.
A time when I will be challenged academically,
And asked to think about a specific subject in a more
detailed and critical way.
But it will also be a time when I challenge myself
physically and emotionally.

Going to university, Lord, has been a dream and an
aspiration of mine
For many years.
I always wanted to see if I was capable of reaching a
higher level,
And now I have that opportunity.
I know it will be hard, Lord.
I know I will be challenged and tested in ways that I
have not experienced before.
I know I will have to write a lot more and do a lot
more reading
Than I have done previously.
I know I will meet people who will have very different
views and opinions to my own.
I know I will experience attitudes, theories, facts, and
myths
That will make me think about the world in a different
way.
I know I am moving towards being an adult, and I will
be challenged
To take more responsibility for my learning

And how I go about researching and gathering information.

As I make this next step in my academic journey,
I ask for your presence to help me and to guide me.
Help me to be open to the information I receive,
Even if it is contrary to what I have always believed.
Help me to stop and calm myself if I feel stressed by this new setting I am in.
Help me not to be afraid to ask for help when I am unsure what to do.
Help me to be kind on myself if I feel overwhelmed
By the amount of work I have to complete.
Help me to be open to new experiences,
Both inside and outside the academic environment.
Help me to grow academically, physically, emotionally, and spiritually
In the days, weeks, months, and years ahead.
Help me to develop and grow,
So that when I leave this place of study I am a more grounded and mature person.
Help me to be able to put my training and my knowledge to good use
To help others and the world around me,
So that with your help I can make a difference to those I meet,
Amen.

7. A prayer for moving away from home

I am moving away from home, Lord, and that thought excites me and scares me.
I moving away and embracing a new setting, a new environment,
And a new beginning in my journey on the road of life.
Moving away from home is something I always knew I would do
At some point in my life
And I am looking forward to the chance to meet new people
And to develop fresh circles of friends.

But it is scary, Lord. There is so much newness that I am going to experience
And I do not know if I am ready for this challenge
And all the changes that are to come.
I worry, Lord, that I will not cope.
I worry that I will not make friends.
I worry that I will feel isolated and on my own.
I worry that I will not know what to do when the day does not go according to plan,
And I encounter situations that I have never had to deal with before
Without the safety network of close family and friends around
To help and to guide me.

Lord, as I prepare myself for this new stage in my life,
I ask for your comfort and reassurance to surround me.

Help me, Lord, to have the wisdom and confidence to step out of the setting
I know so well, and embrace this new place where I am going.
Help me to have the inner strength to ask for help when I need it.
Help me to look for opportunities where I can develop and grow.
Help me not to be scared when I experience a new situation.
Help me to always keep you in the centre of everything I do.

You, Lord, have always been the constant light in my life,
And I am so thankful that you have guided me on my journey so far.
I know that this move will be hard, but it will also be exciting.
I know there will be days of laughter and joy,
But I also know there will be days of tears and sadness.
And that is OK,
Because that is how I will grow as a person.
Throughout all that I go through as I make this next progression in my life
I ask that you be with me to strengthen me, to support me, to inspire me, to love me, And to reassure me as I gain the experiences I need
To help me to grow more into the person you have planned me to be
This day and in the future,
Amen.

8. A prayer for new places and new beginnings

Making changes, Lord, has always caused me to feel a mix of emotions.
I feel excited about the new opportunities and the chance to meet new people.
There is the potential for new experiences.
But I am scared, Lord.
What if I don't fit in?
What if no one wants to talk to me?
What if people don't like me and ignore me?

Sometimes staying with what I know is easier.
I feel safer, Lord, not making changes.
I like the familiar day-to-day routine of what I have known for a long time.
It is comforting, it is relaxing, and it is safe.
Above all, Lord, there is limited risk to my being hurt or upset.

But, Lord, what I have now is not satisfying.
It is too mundane.
If I look closely, it is becoming harder for me to motivate myself.
Where I am now does not excite me,
Not the way it used to do.
I also hear your voice in my head, telling me to trust and believe.
I know you are asking me to trust you,
To take steps into the unknown,
To try new places, and to make fresh beginnings.

I have never seen myself as a confident risk-taker.
I have always tried to hide away in the background.
But, Lord, if you are asking me to change and move on,
Give me courage and belief.
Help me have the courage that Jesus had when he said,
'Not my will, but yours.'
Always it should be your will, Lord, that is done.
But it can be so difficult to let that happen.
It probably is one of the scariest moments in life,
To go out into the unknown and follow you
Without the safety net of the familiar around me.

I know, Lord, you are always with me.
Give me peace and calmness to face new challenges.
When I am unsure what to do, guide me with your grace and wisdom
To make the right choices, to find answers, and to not hide away and be scared.
If I make mistakes, Lord, and I know I will,
Help me to learn from my errors and not beat myself up because I have made them.
Help me to be the person you believe I can be.
Even if I am not convinced, I can be that person.
Lord, continue to be the rock that I can lean on for support
And be the warm, loving blanket that wraps around me
To provide reassurance in difficult times.
Help me feel your loving presence in this new place as I begin this new journey,
Amen.

9. A thankful prayer for the gift of life and special moments

Lord, thank you for the gift of life,
For the precious moments I share in,
For the people who are around me who I love.
I see such joy in the faces of the people around me,
The hope and excitement of the days to come,
The wondrous expectation of new experiences.
Bless my friends and family, Lord.
Bless each moment that we experience.
In the hard times give us, and those we love,
Strength, courage, and confidence.
In good times help us to be thankful and gracious.
At all times, Lord, help us to think of you,
And to give you praise and thanks.
For you are always with us, Lord.
You are the same today, tomorrow, and forever.
Thank you, Lord, for being you,
And for always being with us,
Amen.

10. A birthday prayer

Today is my birthday, Lord,
And I am so excited about this day.
Every year I look forward to this special moment in the year,
The day I came into the world,
And our relationship began.
You, Lord, have given me so much,
And I have been blessed by you in so many different ways.

Life has not always been easy, Lord.
There have been dark days,
And days of tears and frustration.
But there have been days of sunshine,
When the joy and laughter I experienced
Left me feeling my heart could burst with delight.

As I celebrate another birthday,
Help me to enjoy this day.
Help me to make it a day that I will remember for the rest of my life.
Help me to share this day with the people who I love the most.
And, Lord, help me to keep you in the centre of this day.
Remind me to give thanks to you
For all the amazing gifts that you have given to me,
And all the love and peace you send to me
This day and always,
Amen.

11. A prayer for a loving relationship

Thank you, Lord, thank you.
I have found love, and I was never sure that love
would happen for me.
I have wanted someone to love me for who I am and
how I am.
I know you love me, Lord, and that helps a lot.
But what I have been hoping would happen
Is to have someone in my life to share life with and
do things with.

So many people have come into my life and have
tried to control it.
They have stripped away my identity.
I have moulded myself into what they wanted me to
be,
And not what you wanted me to be.
But now, Lord, I have found someone who loves me
for me.
They love my quirks, my personality, the good, and
the bad of me.
They want me to be me and to grow and develop
with them.
It feels like a real partnership,
A togetherness that I have not experienced before,
but always dreamed about.

Life isn't always easy. We disagree.
We don't always see every situation the same way.
But that is OK because it helps us both to develop.
Compromising, and trying to see the other person's
point of view,
Helps me to have a better understanding.

It helps me to become a better person.
And because we love each other, we support each other.
We talk, we share, we hug, and we work and enjoy life together.

Lord, keep our love growing.
Help us to continue to work together, to learn together,
To develop and experience more of life together.
And help us to keep you in the centre of everything we do.
Wherever we go, wherever life takes us, whatever life gives us,
Give us the courage, strength, and confidence to know what we should do.
And to reflect our love for you and each other in all the situations of our lives,
Amen.

12. A prayer for marriage

Today is the day I get married, Lord.
I have been waiting for this moment for a long time.
Finally, the day is here.
I feel nervous, I feel excited,
I feel happy, but there is some fear, Lord.
On this day in front of you and our friends and family,
I commit to sharing my life with my beloved.
I commit to looking after them and cherishing each
moment we share.
That excites me, Lord. That fills me with so much joy
and hope.

Lord, I ask you to bless our relationship, bless our
partnership, bless our marriage.
Bless each experience we have together.
Help us to keep talking to one another and keep us
sharing,
Whether we have good times or bad times,
Whether we are rich or struggle to make ends meet.
Whether we have children or are not blessed with
children,
Help us to openly share our thoughts, our concerns,
our hopes, and our dreams.

When we disagree, speak to us through our mist of
anger and frustration.
Help us to find answers and find a compromise that
works for both of us.
And when that can't happen, Lord, help us to stay
together
And find love and the understanding of each other's
points of view.

Stay with us, Lord, even if at times through our stubbornness we turn away from you.
Keep us, strong, Lord. Give us inspiration, wisdom, and courage in the difficult times.
Keep us calm, Lord, when life does not go according to plan.
Help us to be imaginative and creative in finding solutions
To the challenges that come our way.

Lord, you have so much love for us.
You have so much compassion and understanding.
Help me and my beloved to show each other that love, that compassion,
And that understanding, as we journey on the path of life together,
Amen.

13. A prayer for a marriage break-up

Lord, my heart and soul feel broken.
I feel a loss and an emptiness that do not feel as if
they can be repaired.
For years I had certainty. I had a sure and stable
foundation in my marriage.
But now it is over, and we have separated.
I feel an overwhelming sadness and uncertainty
about what I should do next.

Most days, Lord, I focus on the past.
I look to see where it went wrong,
What I could or should have done differently,
And I wonder if that would have made a difference.
I know that not everything in our relationship was
perfect,
But I thought we were OK.
I really did not see this happening.
And now I feel shattered, inside and out.
I am trying to find answers on my own,
But that is just making me feel worse,
And right now, Lord, I don't feel like I can keep going
on my own.

As I take this time to talk with you, Lord,
I realise that you are the voice I have not stopped
hearing.
I realise that I am not on my own, for you are there
beside me.
I know that you do not place me in situations that I
cannot cope with,
So speak to me, Lord, and guide me in what I should
do next.

Calm my heart and my mind.

I need your help. I need you to be my guiding light.
I need you to be my protector, my comforter, my
friend.
I need you to lead me, Lord, and guide me to find
support.
I need you to help me to be honest and open, to be
candid, and to be fair.

Help me to stop looking to the past to find answers.
Help me to listen to you and not try to do everything
on my own.
Help me to recognise and accept the support you
send.
Help me to keep calm and positive.
In the days, weeks, and months ahead,
Help me to know what it is you want me to do.
Help me to find strength, wisdom, and courage.
Help me to make good decisions and wise choices.

And, Lord, be a comfort and strength to my family.
Help them to hear your voice.
Let them feel your grace, your peace, and your love.
Be with them as our lives change.
Comfort them when they feel sad.
Help us all, Lord, to find the positives in this situation,
So that we can all become better servants of your
living, loving presence,
Amen.

14. A prayer for a family during the break-up of a marriage

Lord, at this time of so much change and so much uncertainty
I need to take time to think of my family and what the separation means for them.
Help me in this busy and challenging time that is before me,
To think of the people around me who I love and who are affected by the separation.
Let them feel your grace, your peace, and your love.
Be with them as our lives change.
Comfort them when they feel sad.
Help them to feel they will always be loved and treasured.
Help me to show that my love for them will never change,
And that they will always be the centre of my life.
Help them to know they can always turn to me
For guidance, support, encouragement, advice, and forgiveness
When life does not always go according to plan.
Stay close to all of us, Lord, and be our constant companion, guide, and friend
As we follow our life's path into the future that you have planned for us all,
Amen.

15. A prayer for a single life

Lord, I want to thank you that I am single.
So often, I am asked about being in a relationship.
Am I not lonely?
Do I not want someone to share intimate moments?
And my answer, Lord, is that I already have that person.
I have you, Lord.
I have my faith.
If I need help, I call to you.
If I feel sad, I talk to you and ask you for your help and guidance.
If I don't know what I should do,
I have a conversation with you
And we openly discuss what I should do.
I don't always hear your voice when we speak.
I don't always know straight away what I should do in particular situations.
But, having spent time with you,
I know what I need to do is to stop,
Be calm, be still, and be in your presence.

And then, Lord, there are my friends and my family.
I am so blessed, Lord, to have so many people around me who love and support me.
You have guided me, Lord, to create my own social network.
A group of people who I can trust in
And who help me to never feel alone.

Lord, you mean so much to me
And you have provided so generously for me in so many ways.

Saying thank you does not seem enough of an acknowledgement.
So, help me, Lord, to sing your praises.
To reflect the love you have for my friends and family and for me.
Let the power of your Holy Spirit pour out from me,
Into the people I meet all the days of my life,
Amen.

16 A prayer for retirement

Lord, today I leave work for the final time.
I have reached the day when I retire.
It feels like the end of an era.
The days, the weeks, the months, and the years of routine
Have come to an end.

Retirement is a time that I have thought about with mixed feelings for years.
Retiring excites me, Lord.
It is a time when I can do something different.
But I also feel apprehensive.
I am not entirely sure what I should do next.

Over the years, Lord,
We have shared so many experiences.
You have helped me to achieve so much.
You have helped me to learn so many different skills.
I have achieved more than I would have thought possible.
I have had the opportunity to be part of a team.
I have met wonderful people and shared in the life experiences
Of my friends and colleagues.
And the experiences and journeys they have been on
Have helped to shape my life's journey and deepened my experiences.

But tomorrow I begin a different journey.
A new chapter in my life will start,
And I will begin a new daily routine.
I am scared, Lord.
Work gave me a role.
I had a purpose.
I belonged to a time and place.
I worry that I will lose the identity that being
employed gave me.

Lord, help me to embrace this next phase in my life.
Help me to look forward with hope and optimism,
And not with fear and regret.
Help me to use the skills and gifts you have given
me
In a new way and in a new place.
Help me to find a new identity and a new role for
myself.
Help me to listen and to learn.
Help me to be gracious and humble.
Help me to keep you in the centre of the next chapter
of my life.
Above all, Lord, help me to enjoy my retirement,
And to make my days of winter
As fulfilling and as rewarding as all the days that
have gone before,
Amen.

17. Thank you for being there, Lord

Heavenly Father, my life feels so busy.
I have so many thoughts, fears, and concerns each day.
And each one takes up so much of my time and energy.
I forget, Lord, that you are in each moment of my life.
You are the living, loving presence
That upholds me and gives me strength.
You, Lord, are the presence that guides and supports me.
Whether I am celebrating, grieving, troubled,
Or living in the hope of better times ahead,
You are there with me.
Continue to be in each and every moment of my life, Lord.
Help me to find rest, hope, and love,
For everything that I have to face,
Amen.

18. Help me cope with change

In an ever-changing world, Lord,
I sometimes find it hard to cope.
So much of what I took for granted has changed.
Friends are no longer around.
I don't get as much time with my family as I used to.
Their lives are so busy,
And I really don't want to trouble them with my problems.
More often now I feel on my own.
Help me, Lord.
Tell me what I should do.
Speak to me, Lord,
And help me to recognise and accept the support you send.
Help me to keep calm and positive
In this forever-altering world,
Amen.

19. A prayer about music

Heavenly Father, so many feelings come over me
each time I listen to music.
Sometimes I feel happy. Sometimes I feel sad.
Sometimes I feel inspired. Sometimes I feel
reassured.
Sometimes I feel energised and can achieve
anything I put my heart and soul into.
Other times I just want to sit still and feel the music
and words wash over me.

As I have progressed on my life journey
I have heard songs and listened to music that has
meant so much to me.
Each piece of music is special.
Each word that has been written has been carefully
planned,
So that the sentiment expressed is heartfelt and
meaningful.
These precious songs often contain the words and
feelings that I want to express,
But so often find hard to say at the right time.
So please hear my thoughts, Lord, and feel what I
feel as I listen to music.
And help me to listen better to you,
Amen.

20. Help me to listen

There is often so much noise in this world
That I miss the most important sounds.
I do not hear the quiet requests for help.
I do not see the needs of the people around me.
I am dazzled by bright lights and loud voices.
Maybe the only time that I pay attention to you
Is when I see the dramatic, the thunder, the lightning.
But you are there, Lord, in all the situations of my
life.
Help me, Lord, to hear and see you more clearly.
Help me to know what it is you want me to do.
Help me to be a better person in all aspects of my
life,
And with all the people I know and meet.
Help me to be more like you
And to reflect and show more of you in my words
and actions,
Amen.

21. A prayer

Thank you for my dog

Lord, thank you for the dog you have brought into my life
And for all the unconditional love and affection that they provide to me.
I love their cute face and the way they look at me.
I love how their character and personality have developed
As we have got to know one another.
Having something to look after, to care for, and to nurture
Has helped give my life a new sense of purpose, direction, and energy.
Having a dog has encouraged me to go out more.
It can help me to meet new people and to engage in the world around me.

I know they will be waiting for me when I wake up in the morning,
Demanding some attention, some food, something to drink,
And maybe even a run outside to loosen their limbs for the day ahead.
I know they will be waiting for me when I come home from a tiring day
Or from a time of fun with family or friends.
I know they will be ready for me to speak with and to listen to me
As I replay the day I have had.
They will not judge me,

And I know, Lord, that I can confide in them all that is
happening in my life,
Just as I can always talk to you, and they will accept
me just as I am.
When I feel sad and I have down days,
They sense my mood and come to me to give me a
cuddle.
They tell me in their own unique way that they are
there to support me.

I feel blessed, Lord, that you have entrusted me
To look after this lovely animal that has come into my
life.
Give me the creativity to find ways in which
I can help their mind and their body to develop.
Give me the patience not to overreact
When they do something I would rather they had not
done.
Give me the energy I need to go out with them
Even when I have had a long, tiring day.
Give me the knowledge I need to help me to know
when they are unwell.
Help me to show the love that is in my heart
So that I can let them know how much they mean to
me.
Help me to be the best guardian and friend of the
animal you have given to me,
So that together we can be a living and loving
example of your presence in our lives,
Amen.

22. A prayer

Thank you for my cat

Thank you, Lord, for my feline friend.
For the joy they provide to me each day.
For their energy and their infectious presence.
For the gift of unconditional love that they bestow on me each day
From the time I wake up in the morning until the time I go to bed.
Sometimes they even join me in sedate slumber as we relax our bodies and minds.

There are days, Lord, when my cat will disappear for hours on end.
They will go out and explore your world
And I pray that they are safe and not getting into trouble.
When they return I give thanks that you have brought them safely back to me.
I also give thanks when they don't bring me back any unwanted gifts.

Having a feline friend in my life
Has helped me to develop a real sense of partnership.
I often feel it is me and them together with you, Lord, journeying through life.
Sharing the ups and the downs.
Talking through the events of the day,
And making plans together for the next part of the journey.
We sense when the other needs a hug and a cuddle.

We sense when we need to spend a quiet, cosy
night together.
We sense when we need some time apart, having
our own adventures,
But knowing we will reunite soon, and continue
developing
The bond of love and affection that you, Lord, have
helped us to create.

Thank you, Lord, for this chance for me to have this
special relationship.
Help me to be ever mindful and alert to their needs.
Help me to watch, to listen, to nurture, and to protect
The feline friend you have entrusted to me.
Give me the wisdom and the courage to help them to
grow and develop
Just as you had planned them to do.
Help me to show the love that is in my heart
So that I can let them know how much they mean to
me.
Help us both to be a living and loving example of
your presence in our lives
As we continue to enjoy all that your world has to
offer,
Amen.

23. A prayer for speaking with God

Lord, it is always good to talk with you.
You are always around, whatever the time of day,
To listen and to help.
Sometimes while I am spending time with you,
I get a thought in my head.
A lightbulb moment, if you like …
'Ah, this is what I should do.'
The thought is clear, and I know what I should do
next.

Other times I get a feeling about situations.
On some occasions, it is a good, positive feeling,
An instinct that you are sending me in a particular
direction,
Because that is what you want me to do.
Sometimes I get a sad feeling.
I worry that what you are asking me to do will be too
difficult.
I will not be able to succeed.
Whatever the situation is,
I know you will assist me, Lord.
I know you will encourage me to represent you
cheerfully
And do the task the way you want me to do it.
If you ask me to step out of my comfort zone,
I pray you will help me to control my nervousness
and fear
And not let my worries control me.
Lord, continue to speak with me.
So that with your help, I can be the person you want
me to be,
Amen.

24. Following God's call

Lord, when you called me to follow you,
You told me to love you with all my heart,
With all my soul, and with all my mind.
And you told me to love my neighbour as I love
myself.
Lord, today I ask that you continue to help me to love
you
And to love my neighbour.
To put what you want me to do above what I want to
do.
To reach out and help.
To shine brightly for you in my daily life,
So that through my words and my actions
I can truly be a light of your eternal glory,
Amen.

25. Help me to do more

Too often I do not remember to think of you
Or to talk to you when I see the difficulties in my life
Or in my local community.
You have given me a place in which I can work, rest,
and play.
And I ask that you bless my friends and my
neighbours.

Thank you for the conversations I have with the
people I meet.
For the opportunities you give me
To be a good friend and neighbour.
The opportunities that I have to listen to others,
To offer help, support, and prayer.
I ask that you bless my daily tasks
And my daily interactions with the people around me.
Let my words, actions, and prayers reflect your
teaching,
Amen.

26. Being in God's presence

It is good to come into your presence, Lord, and sing your praises.
It is good that I can spend time with friends and family, reflecting on you,
Learning more about you.
Resting and restoring, through song and music,
My spiritual soul and my earthly body.

So much, Lord, can be expressed through the lyrics of a song.
So much can be felt in the melodies of a piece of music.
Lord, come here, into my singing,
Into my prayers, and into my life.
Help me to make a special place for you
And to hold you close this day and always,
Amen.

27. The candle prayer

I light a candle as a sign of my love and trust in you.
I light a candle as a sign of the hope that I need each day
To help me through the challenges I face.
As I watch the candle flicker and burn,
I am reminded that you are the light of the world.
I am reminded of your constant eternal presence,
Which encourages, inspires, and leads me.
I am reminded that, whatever situation I experience,
You will be there to help guide and support me.

You, Lord, are the light that burns in the darkness.
Be the light in the dark places of my life
And help me in the situations that cause me stress and anxiety.
Strengthen and guide me when I feel lost and confused
And in need of encouragement.
Give me the wisdom to find answers
And the courage and confidence to follow where you lead.
Help me to accept the advice and support
That will enable me to grow and develop into the person you always need me to be.
Help me to keep your light burning in the centre of my life
To illuminate the path you have called me to follow.
Help me to always see your light wherever I journey in life
And to constantly feel your loving and supporting presence all the days of my life,
Amen.

28. A prayer for calm and renewal

Lord, I need a time of renewal in my life.
A time to reflect. A time to be calm and still.
A time to pause and assess my life.
A time to plan and to structure what it is I want to do.

But I don't know how to do these things.
I don't know how to stop being busy.
I don't know how to be calm and still.
I don't know how to reflect and plan.
I only know to do things and be in the moment,
And, right now, that doesn't seem fulfilling.
Life does not feel as much fun as I think it could be,
and every task is an effort.

Help me to find joy in doing things.
Help me to find tasks that make a difference.
Help me to let go of things I do that are no longer
rewarding.
Help me to find your peace and love,
And to be renewed in your grace and inspired by
your spirit.
Let me work for you and not for myself.
And let me bring pleasure into the lives of the people
I meet,
Amen.

29. A prayer for worry

Lord, one of the hardest things I find to do is to let go.
I take the worries of the day and hold on to them.
I brood over them.
My mind becomes totally focused on the stresses of the day.
I become so obsessed by worry
That it affects my ability to enjoy the people and the things around me.
But you have told me to trust in you.
To ask plainly and simply for what I need and it will be granted.
So I ask, Lord, for you to help me.
Help me to place into your hands what I cannot control.
Help me to be quiet in my mind, so that I can hear from you.
And speak to me, Lord,
Let me know what I should do and how I should respond.
Help me to trust in you, Lord, and in the people around me.
I pray this prayer in your name,
Amen.

30. A prayer for anger

Why do I get so angry and frustrated, Lord?
Every time I hear about that situation, that person,
I get agitated inside.
My words and actions become defensive.
I am annoyed, and my anger and frustration come to
the surface.
I find it hard to let go, Lord.
How do I let go, Lord?
Teach me and tell me what I should do.
Calm me, and help me to let your loving presence
Come into my body, mind, and soul.
I may not be able to forgive, Lord,
Not in the way you always can.
But help me to be a better person,
So that I can be more like you in the situations that
cause me the most hurt and pain,
Amen.

31. A prayer for light

You sent to me, Lord, the light of the world
And you told me that no matter how dark the world becomes
Your light would shine brightly.
Your light brings love and joy.
It brings reassurance and forgiveness.
It brings enduring peace and everlasting hope.
In you, Lord, I find strength and guidance.
Help me to trust in your light.
Give me the courage and the confidence to walk the path
You have put me on,
So that I can achieve the goals you have planned for me.
I pray this prayer in your name,
Amen.

32. A prayer for help in dark times

I find it hard, Lord, to have a positive thought.
I feel low, and I have no motivation and confidence.
I am scared to go out because I am worried about
how people will look at me.
They will speak about me behind my back as I walk
down the street.
They will judge me. They will criticise me.
They may not know me, but the voice in my head
Keeps telling me I am a bad person.
And the people I see must see that about me.

Lord, so many voices compete in my head.
Many of the voices are negative, hurtful, and
frightening.
I want the voices to stop, Lord.
I want to feel whole and pure.
I want to feel confident and self-assured.
Can that happen, Lord?
Can I feel positive about myself?
Help me, Lord, to find the answers I seek.
The journey will be hard. It will be emotional, and it
will be painful
And I know that on many occasions I will want to
give up.
I know there are events in my past that I don't want
to revisit,
Events I have tried to put behind me.
But sometimes in the darkness and in the quiet
moments,
Those experiences come back to me.
They scare me and unnerve me.

In those moments, Lord, as I work through the darker parts of my life,
Draw closer to me.
Help me to feel your presence, your grace, your peace.
Keep me, strong, Lord.
Surround me with people who can I lean on for support.
Let your light shine brightly for me, Lord,
Keep it in front of me like a beacon that helps me through the dark times.
And bring me out of the darkness and into your pure, radiant light.
Hold on to me, Lord, and never let me go,
So that I can be one with you forever and ever,
Amen.

33. A prayer for help to be supportive

I want to help, Lord,
I see so much pain and anguish in my friend's life.
I see them struggling to cope with the dark times
they have been through.
I know they want me to help.
They need me to be strong for them.
But I am not sure I know what I should do.
I don't know how I should help.
I am nervous, Lord, and scared I will do the wrong
thing,
Say the wrong word, or act in a way that is not
supportive.
I worry that my words and my actions will cause
harm, not good.
I know, deep down, that I cannot fix what has
happened in the past.

Help me, Lord.
Stop me from giving advice at times when I should
be listening.
Stop me from asking questions or saying unhelpful
phrases.
Stop me from trying to find answers,
When my very presence should be answer enough.
Help me to find words of reassurance and comfort.

Teach me, Lord, that I don't have to speak to make a
significant difference.
Keep me calm when I hear things that upset and
anger me.
Give me courage, confidence, and wisdom, to stay
close

Even when what I see and hear may make me want to run away.
Help me to show your unconditional love, your grace, your mercy,
Your peace, and your forgiveness through simple words and actions.
For in you, Lord, each one of us finds hope and salvation.
Let your eternal love shine through me
So that they can be strengthened and supported in their journey,
Amen.

34. A prayer for using social media

Lord, as I use social media,
Help me to be mindful of how my postings can affect others.
Help me to enjoy my time communicating with friends.
Help me to stay safe and to keep the safety of others I communicate with
In my mind as I write my postings.
Help me to be kind and encouraging with the words I type and the emojis I send.

When I feel angry and frustrated with others,
Help me to stay calm and not post something I will later regret.
When I feel hurt and upset by the comments others have made,
Help me to have the strength to speak with family and friends,
And not keep the hurt building up inside me.
Help me to use social media as a way of reflecting
The qualities of the love, the compassion, and the understanding
That you have asked me to show whenever I speak with people.
Help me this day and always, to make my posts show
The love and kindness that I want people to feel as they journey through life.
Help me to share with others the hope and optimism I have found
Through trusting in you as my friend and companion,
Amen.

35. Thank you for the radio, the television, the Internet, and the telephone

I am grateful, Lord, for the technology that surrounds me.
It is a joy to be able to put on the radio and hear stories being read aloud.
Stories that transport me to a different time and place.
Sometimes the stories move me to a completely different world,
One that is full of adventure, drama, love, and romance.

It is a joy to be able to listen to a wide variety of music.
I love to hear an eclectic mix of rhythms and beats.
Some music I hear energises me and inspires my creative instincts.
Some music I hear helps me revisit a special moment in my life.
Some music I hear calms me and soothes away the worries of the day.
Some music I hear just makes me smile and laugh.

It is a joy to hear accounts from around the world.
To experience different cultures, faiths, and religions.
To open my mind to all the diversity that exists in your amazing world.
Sometimes to even learn of worlds that are far away from my own planet.

It is a joy to watch the creativity of others that has been captured on film.
Bright colours and lights illuminate my television.
A natural world brought closer to me
Through the power of high-performance cameras
That can make me feel as though I really am at one with nature,
Even though I haven't gone outdoors.
The intrigue of a period drama brought to life in glorious technicolour.
And let me not forget the regular dose of my favourite soap opera,
Which keeps me so engaged, episode by episode,
As I see my favourite characters develop.

It is a joy to be able to unite with people from all over the globe through the Internet.
From watching songs performed in a kitchen,
To hearing faith services recorded in a living room,
Technology enables me to come together with hundreds and thousands of people.
It enables me to share experiences in the virtual world.

It is a joy to speak to people on the telephone.
To hear another person's voice and to know that we are not alone.
The phone allows me to connect with friends and family
Wherever they are in the world, at any time of the day or night.
It enables me to use my voice as well as my eyes and ears
So that I can share news

And hear how the world outside my enclosed space is changing.

Through the power of the radio, the television, the Internet, and the phone,
My mind is enriched and my life can feel more connected.
Thank you, Lord, for having given me so many different ways
In which I can stay connected.
Thank you for having provided me with the chance to explore, and
To learn more about the ever-changing and constantly evolving world around me.
Thank you for giving me old friends and new companions
Who I can share these experiences with as I journey through each day.
Most of all, Lord, it is a joy to share these experiences with you,
My risen friend and eternal companion.
It is a joy to share a cup of tea or coffee with you each day as we relax together
And discuss all that I have seen and heard
From all the many forms of communication that you have helped to create
To enable me to stay connected in your world,
Amen.

36. A prayer for a holiday

Lord, as I prepare for my time away on holiday,
I ask for your calming presence to help and to guide.
I have to remember so many things that I have to do
before I go away.
So many jobs I need to complete.
Help me to prioritise each task,
And to be kind to myself for the jobs I don't get done.

In all the preparations for my holiday, Lord,
Help me to look forward to my time away with joy
and happiness in my heart.
Be with me, Lord, as I pack.
Help me to remember the essential things that I have
to take with me.
Help to remember the important documents I need.
Help me to see preparing for the holiday as a time of
fun and not of stress.

Bless my holiday, Lord.
Help me to relax.
Help me to switch off from the stresses and strains of
my daily life.
Help me to renew, to refresh, and to re-energise
myself.
Help me in this time away,
To deepen my bond of love and friendship with those
who mean the most to me.
Help me to meet new people,
To make new friendships,
To enjoy familiar and unfamiliar experiences.
To make new memories that will stay with me all the
days of my life.

And help me to always give praise and thanks to you,
For all that I see, hear, touch, and taste,
As I go on holiday and begin this exciting journey,
Amen.

37. A prayer for the end of spring into summer

The days of spring are coming to an end,
And the time of bright sunny days and days of liquid
sun are before me.

Moving from spring into summer can often be a time
of relaxation.
A time for holidays both at home and further afield,
A time to make the most of the beautiful world that
you have created,
A time for my family and friends to gather and to
share in fun, laughter, and music.
But it can also be a time when I become too hot,
And I may feel very uncomfortable, both during the
day and the night.

In the days to come, help me to stay healthy and to
be sensible.
Help me to remember what I can do to reduce my
body temperature
And to keep myself healthy.
Help me not to take unnecessary risks that can spoil
the opportunities you give me.

As the days get longer and the temperature rises,
I want to ask you to help me to make the most of the
opportunities you give me.
Help me to soak up the experiences that are around
me.
Help me to enjoy the vibrant colours, the sunshine,
and the rain

That will probably come as I move through the summer season to come.

Help me, in this time of relaxation, to see the world around me through your eyes.
Help me to make the most of the times when I can be outside.
Help me to make a fresh album of memories,
Filled with conversations and experiences that will sustain me
Through the seasons to come.
Help me, Lord, to take this time to relax, to be still in your presence,
To be quiet in my surroundings, and to be re-energised by your love,
So that, as the days of summer come to an end,
I am ready to embrace the challenges that are ahead of me,
Amen.

38. A prayer for the end of summer into autumn

Lord, as I come to the end of this summer season,
I give thanks for your presence in all that I have done.
Thank you for the bright, glorious sunny days.
Thank you for the days of liquid sun.
Thank you for the times I have shared with family and friends.
Thank you for the conversations, the fun, and the times of play.
Thank you for being there with me as I created more memories,
Which I can add to the album of life that you have helped me to build.

As I move from the long days of summer to the shorter days of autumn,
Stay with me, Lord.
As the leaves change colour, and the nights close in,
Help me to feel your warm glow in my heart.
Fire me with your spirit, Lord, inspire me with your love,
And help me to forever be the beacon of your light and hope
As I continue on the path of ministry and faith that you have called me to walk,
Amen.

39. A prayer for the end of autumn into winter

Lord, the days of autumn are coming to an end,
And the bitter winds of winter are beginning to blow.
In this time of snow and ice, cold winds and rain, barren trees,
And hibernating animals, I see so much colour and so many bright lights.
I see the seasonal decorations that adorn so many houses and light up the dark sky.
I see the days getting shorter and the nights getting longer.
I see the busyness of the Christmas season as I journey towards Christmas
And then prepare for the beginning of a new year.

The time of winter provides such an array of emotions.
It is a time of reflection,
A time of following familiar traditions,
A time to remember the friends and family who are now in your loving care.

The season of winter often blends together the good and bad moments of life.
There will be times of joy, fun, and laughter, when I can create new memories.
But there will be times of sadness
And times when I feel unwell and not able to accomplish what I want to achieve.
In all the days during this season, let me feel your presence.
Let me experience your loving embrace surrounding me.

Let your healing and your divine grace flow within me.

As I move through winter towards spring, be my companion of light and hope.
Help my mind, my body and my soul to be reset, refreshed, and re-energised
By your Holy Spirit.
Help me to move from winter into spring with the sure and certain knowledge
That we will journey the days, weeks, and months ahead together.
With you at my side, Lord, ready to catch and hold me should I stumble or fall,
I am ready to continue on the path of life in the year ahead,
Amen.

40. A prayer for the end of winter into spring

Lord, I see the yellow daffodils appearing in the garden and along the roadsides,
And I know that the dark days of winter are coming to an end.
The cold rains, harsh winds, ice, and snow are beginning to fade away.
The season of spring is coming into view and a time of newness is near.
I feel the hope of fresh starts and the optimism that is around me,
As the plants and the animals begin to come out of their winter hibernation.

Moving from winter into spring is a time for me to wake up from my own hibernation.
It is a time of preparation.
It is a time of new life, new beginnings, fresh starts, and new opportunities
For me to develop and to grow.
It is a time when I can make plans for the longer days
And the shorter nights that are before me.

But spring is also a time when I am challenged by you.
I am challenged to make a sacrifice and a commitment in your name.
I am challenged to make a difference both in my own life
And in the lives of the people around me.
Yet I don't always know, Lord, what the challenge should be.

I don't always know what I can do either for myself,
or for others,
That would make a difference.

As I prepare for this change in season, I look for your
presence around me.
I look for the message you have for me and the
challenge you have prepared for me.
Speak to me, Lord, and demand more from me.
Challenge me and make me realise that whatever
task you call me to do,
You will provide all I need to achieve the goals you
have set me.
Help me to enjoy the days of springtime and the
beginning of a new journey with you.
Let me be inspired by your love and enriched with
your grace and mercy.
Help me to make decisions in all aspects of my life
That will reflect the love and commitment I have for
you.
Help me in this springtime to show through my words
and actions
What you mean to me, so that all that I do for friends,
family, and strangers
Will be an offering and a sacrifice worthy of your
teachings
And of the life you have asked me to follow,
Amen.

41. A prayer for the seasons

As I have moved through the seasons, Lord, I have seen so much change.
I have seen the changes in the weather.
I have seen the changes in the landscapes around me.
I have seen the changes in the types of birds and other animals
That have appeared in my garden and all around me
As I have walked about the places where I live and work.
But I have also seen changes in my own life.
Changes in my health, and in the health of my family and friends.
Changes in the activities I can do
And in the ways in which I can interact and spend time with others.
Some changes have been lovely and relaxing, and have helped me
To create memories that will enable me to remember special occasions and events.
Other changes ... Well, they have been less welcome,
And have been more physically and emotionally demanding.

Change is inevitable, Lord, and I do accept that fact.
But one thing that never changes is you.
Whether it is raining or snowing,
Whether it is windy or icy, or whether it is hot or cold,
You are there beside me.
I cannot control the weather. I cannot control the changes in the seasons.

I cannot completely control what will happen in my
life each day,
But I can control who I turn to every day as my
companion in life.

Journeying through the seasons is like the journey
through life.
I will have days when I am in the springtime of my
life with so much ahead of me.
I will have days of summer, which may feel carefree,
But which can often have challenges that I need to
face
To help me to grow in my journey on the road of life.
I will have days of autumn, when so much in my life
will change,
And that will be not only exciting but also a bit scary
and unnerving.
I will have days of winter when I cannot do as much
as I want to do
Because my body and my mind will not be as active
as they were in the past.

Throughout each one of these days,
I thank you for your continued love and unconditional
presence.
I thank you that you have challenged me
And have encouraged me to think about situations in
a new way.
I thank you that you have helped me to grow
physically, emotionally, and spiritually.
I thank you that you will always be with me
In the spring, summer, autumn, and winter of my
days.

I thank you for guiding me, for encouraging me, for forgiving me, for challenging me, For inspiring me, for loving me, and for helping me to be a better person,
This day and all the days of my life.
I thank you for all that I have experienced, and for helping me
To create an album of memories,
With which you have shaped me into the person I am today,
Amen.

42. A prayer for the climate

Lord, you created a perfect world,
A world that provides for all.
But it is being ruined,
And I know I have played a part in that change.
I see the climate becoming too hot, sea levels rising,
and ice caps melting …
Your world burning, and plants, animals, and human
life being destroyed,
And I am scared and frightened about the future.

Some people tell me the changes are no different to
how they have been in the past.
There have always been variations in the weather.
There have always been earthquakes, floods, and
fires.
Yet this feels different. The changes are too extreme,
And the frequency of these natural disasters is
increasing.
They are happening in too many places in your world
to be the normal cycle of life.

In the midst of this climatic disaster
I need to hear your voice. I need to know what I
should do.
I know, Lord, that I can recycle my waste.
I can reduce how much plastic I use,
And I can switch the lights off when I am not in the
room.
But somehow, Lord, that does not seem to be
enough.
Your world continues to be destroyed.
Everything around me is changing.

You, Lord, have given me so much.
You have provided for me in so many different ways,
And I have taken for granted everything you have
given me.
Forgive me, Lord. Speak to me and guide me.
Help me to make changes to the way I live.
Help me to understand that small changes make a
difference.
Help me to be a better guardian of everything you
have entrusted to me.
Remind me, Lord, to always include your earth and
everything in it in my prayers.
And to understand that in caring for your world, I am
showing my love for you,
Just as you have always loved me,
Amen.

43. A prayer for unwell friends

Lord, my friend is unwell, and I feel helpless that I cannot step in
And take away their pain and suffering.
I feel frustrated, Lord, and at times I am not sure what I can do to help.
When I am distracted, when I am worried,
And when I cannot clear my head of the noise around me,
I don't always turn to you for help.
I try and find answers on my own.
But you, Lord, can work miracles,
And you can perform wonders far beyond my comprehension if I ask for your help.

Lord, I ask you for help.
Help me to see and hear your presence.
Send your divine power and grace into the physical and mental well-being
Of all who I know are in need of your healing presence.
In a few moments of quiet,
I speak aloud to you the names of those who are in my heart.

Be their light, Lord.
Be their hope, be their guardian, be their protector, and be their friend.
And help all of us, Lord, to know your love, peace, and understanding,
This day and always,
Amen.

44. A prayer for charitable giving

Lord, another request has been made of me to give money to charity.
I want to give, Lord. I want to play my part and to help people and animals in need.
But, Lord, my resources are limited.
I cannot give to all the charities that my heart feels I should support.
Help me, Lord,
Help me to know which charities I should give to.
Help me to divide the money I want to give,
So that all the good causes I want to support can carry on their much-needed work.
Help me to also remember
That my support does not always need to be financial.
Although I may not be able to give as much as I want to,
Or maybe not even as much as I used to give,
Remind me to keep every charitable organisation in my prayers.
You, Lord, can do so much more than I can possibly imagine.
But in order for you to do your work,
I need to ask for your help.
So, in a time of quiet,
I pause and speak to you about all the charities that mean so much to me.

Bless all the work they do.
Help them to have the resources they need to make a difference,
Whether that be human, financial, or material help.

Give all charitable organisations courage, wisdom,
and spiritual strength,
So that in the darkest of times,
All who are in need will see the light of your
everlasting love and hope,
Burning brightly as a source of encouragement.
And bless all, Lord, who are called to do your work,
In this country and around the world,
Amen.

45. A prayer for forgiveness

Forgive me, Lord. I know what I said and did was wrong.
I can probably make excuses
And explain in detail what led to my words and actions.
But that really isn't going to help.
I don't feel good about myself.
I feel sad, and as though I have let myself down.
And I have let you down.
Help me, Lord.
Help me to behave better in the situations that frustrate me.
Help me to be calmer and find better responses.
Help me not to react with the words and actions
That will hurt the people around me.
Help me to be more tolerant and understanding.
Help me to be more like you in situations that cause me the most stress.
I pray for your loving grace and patience to enter my life,
Amen.

46. A prayer for trusting in God

In ever-changing and uncertain times,
Remind me, Lord,
That you have gone through my life experiences
before me,
And are ready to help me.

You, Lord, have helped shape my past.
You have planned out my future,
And you encourage me to step forward with you in
confidence.
As I face the day-to-day challenge of my life,
Help me to approach each change with optimism
and courage.

I sometimes don't think I have much to offer, Lord,
But I know you have given me a gift and a talent I
can share.
Help me to find and use the talents you have given
me.
Encourage me to walk forward in my faith,
And know that as I do walk with you,
I will bring alive the hopes and dreams that you have
for me.
For you, Lord, do not change. You remain with me,
So I do not have to fear anything or anyone,
As you are at hand to bless and support me,
Amen.

47. A prayer for illness

Lord, I don't feel well, but I don't know what is wrong.
I am having tests, and I am scared of the unknown.
Although I know you are with me, Lord,
It is not easy for me to remember to look for you.
The fear of uncertainty is taking over my thoughts.

Lord, help my heart, mind, body, and soul
To be calmed by your love.
Help me to stop worrying about the things I cannot
control.
Help me to trust in you and in the doctors and the
medical staff.
Lord, you have guided me to find the help I need.
Be near me, Lord, and give me strength and
courage.
Help me to have confidence in you
And in those who are trying to help.
Let your light of eternal life shine for me
As I journey this path,
Amen.

48. A prayer for terminal illness

Why did this have to happen, Lord?
Why did my body have to begin to fail and I why did I become so ill?
That now there is no hope for me?
I have been told my illness is terminal. There is nothing more that can be done.
I feel angry. I feel frustrated. I feel hurt and alone in my inner turmoil.
My heart is breaking, Lord, and I cry out to you for help.
I cry out to you for answers to why this is happening.
I look for you in the midst of my anguish, but in my tears I cannot clearly see you.

But something inside me tells me you are there.
You are at my bedside at times when I am feeling tired and unwell.
You are in the oxygen that I breathe in and the medication I take
To help me ease the discomfort.
You are in the medical staff providing my care and support.
You are in the hands that I hold in the darkness.
You are in the words that are spoken to me to provide some comfort and support.
You will be there with me when I return to your care
To be looked after by your heavenly angels, and by those who have gone before me.
You are there as we spend time together
Until I am reunited with all my family and friends in your eternal kingdom.

Lord, I understand that becoming ill is part of the natural evolution of life.
But that does not always help me
To overcome the fears I have about what lies before me.
What I am going through is changing my life,
And it is changing the lives of the people around me.
Soon I will no longer be able to hold the hand of my loved ones,
For I will be resting in your glory.

Comfort me, Lord, in my sickness.
Give me the strength and reassurance that I will never be alone.
Help me to feel your soothing presence surrounding me.
Help me to know the love that flows into me from all my family and friends,
And from all those who are caring for me.
You, Lord, have gone before me. You provide the rod and the staff that comfort me.
You provide the light of the world that leads me.
You walk the path of life beside me,
And you have promised to always be with me
At each step I make along the road of life.

Hold me close, Lord, and never let me go,
For it is you who I depend on now and always,
Amen.

49. A prayer for having surgery

Lord, I have been told I need to have an operation.
I have never had surgery before, and I don't know
what to expect.
The doctors have explained what will happen,
But it is not always easy for me to take it all in.
Be with me, Lord, and give me the courage I need.
Bless the doctors, the nurses, and the medical teams
Who will look after me, during the operation and
afterwards.
When I feel nervous and scared, surround me with
your love.
Help me to feel your presence, Lord,
And give me the courage and the strength for this
operation.
Help me to have the confidence to ask for help and
to explain how I feel.
Help to know that you will never leave me
And that you will always be with me in everything I
experience,
This day and always,
Amen.

50. A prayer for an unwell child

Lord, my child is not well,
And I am a long way from their side.
I want to be there with them,
To hold their hand,
To tell them how much I care about them,
And how much I love them.

Even though there are many miles between us,
They are my first thought in the morning,
And my last thought at the end of the day.
Lord, I find it difficult to know what I should say to
you.
I find it difficult to pray to you.
But I know that you know what is in my heart.
You know the feelings that I have,
Which I cannot always put into words.

Be with my child, Lord.
No matter how old they get,
They will always be my child.
Comfort them, Lord, during their treatment.
Give them strength and courage when times are
hard.
Surround them with your healing arms
And your awesome presence.
Guide the medical staff who are treating them.
Help them to get better, Lord,
To be restored to full strength.
Keep them safe for me, Lord.
And help me to find the words
To let them know I am thinking of them,
This day and always. Amen.

51. A prayer for friends at difficult times

Lord, I ask you to bless our friends today.
Bless their days together.
Make each moment special and memorable.
Make each hour they share together
Contain a lifetime of love and affection.
Make each one of their conversations
Show the love they have for each other.
Help them, in the days they spend together,
To reveal how much they care about one another.
To show, through words and actions,
The love and support that will never fade away.

We never know what the future holds.
We never know what will happen, moment by
moment.
But you, Lord, have counted the days we have.
You know our past, our present, and our future.
And you walk the path of life with us,
Your rod and staff are always present to comfort, to
strengthen, and to guide.

Help our friends, Lord, to feel your grace and power.
Help them to feel your love and peace.
Help them to know that you will always be with them
In the bright days, and in the darker times.

And help them, Lord, to know we are there to
support them.
Help them to know that our love, our thoughts, and
our prayers, flow from us to them.
Let all our friends know that they are always in our
hearts and minds, this day and always. Amen

52. A prayer for the family or friend of a person having surgery

I feel helpless, Lord,
I feel there is nothing for me to do in these hours,
while the operation is taking place.
Everything is in your hands, Lord,
And in the hands of the surgeons, anaesthetists, and nurses.
These are difficult times for me, Lord.
I have no control. There is nothing I can say or do that will make a difference.
But there is speaking to you, Lord, that can help.

Be with the medical staff, Lord.
Bless them in their work.
Give the surgeons wisdom to see what must be done.
Keep them calm and confident if things do go according to plan.
Bless the anaesthetists as they look after my loved one during the operation.
Bless the nursing staff and the medical assistants
As they support the surgical team in theatre and in the recovery room.
And above all, Lord, keep my loved one safe.
Bring them through this operation.
Be with them in the operating theatre
And in the recovery room.
When they feel pain and discomfort, bring them peace.
And help me, Lord, to be a calm and supporting presence

In the hours, days, and weeks following the
operation,
Amen.

53. A prayer for the sudden loss of a loved one

I feel angry, Lord.
I feel you have let me down.
You have taken away my loved one from me.
I don't understand why.
There was no warning. There was no time to prepare.
We were enjoying our days together.
We had so many plans.
There were so many things we wanted to do together.
And suddenly they are gone.
And I am alone.
Our plans are unfulfilled memories.

Why did you do this, Lord?
Why did you call them to you?
I wasn't ready to let them go.
I want to be angry with you.
I am angry, I am hurt, I am confused,
And I am scared.
In all the emotions I feel, I fear the unknown.
A life without my loved one cut abruptly short.
I don't know what I should do next, Lord.
I don't know how I can carry on with life's journey without the other part of me.

Help me find some peace in my body, mind, and soul.
Help me to find the courage and the strength to carry on.
I may never understand why this happened,

But help me to find the forgiveness in my heart that
you have for me.
And take good care of my loved one,
So that one day we will be reunited together with you
In your eternal kingdom,
Amen.

54. A prayer for the loss of a loved one

Lord, my heart is so heavy,
I really don't know what words I can say to you right
now.
I feel a piece of my heart, my soul, my very body,
has gone today,
And I don't know if it will ever come back.

I want to give thanks for the life of my loved one,
To thank you for the times we shared.
But right now I can't express that.
I just feel empty and lost.
You know me, Lord.
You know what I need,
Speak to me, Lord. Help me find the comfort I need.
Help me to find the strength to get through the next
few days and weeks,
Amen.

55. A prayer for the loss of a sister

Lord, today will be hard, and I need your help.
Surround me with your love,
And stay close to me as I pass my sister over to your care.
My heart is filled with sadness, and I miss her so much.
But she would not want me to be sad,
And I have so much joy for all that we shared together.
Help me to remember those precious moments that we enjoyed together.
Help me to remember the words of encouragement she spoke to me.
Help me to recall the memories that we created,
Which provide a source of happiness even in the darkness.
I know, Lord, that my sister is with you and that you have ignited
An eternal light for her, which burns brightly in your kingdom.
Help me to see her light as I journey on the road of life.
Help me to feel her spirit as she walks alongside me.
Help me to hear her voice in the good days and the hard times that are ahead.
And take care of her, Lord.
Look after her and keep her safe,
Until the day when we reunite and celebrate together in your glorious presence,
Amen.

56. A prayer for the loss of a brother

Today, Lord, will be hard,
Because I not only give back to you my brother,
But I also give back my friend,
Who I shared so much with over the many years we
have been together.
There was so much of life that we shared.
We did not always get on. We argued and we fought
sometimes.
But he was my brother,
And we almost always found a way to reunite the
bond we shared.
We looked out for each other.
We were always there for each other in the good
times and in the sad times.
Now my heart is filled with sadness, and I miss him
so much.
I know he would not want me to be sad.
He would want me to remember the precious
moments that we enjoyed together.
He would want me to remember the words of
encouragement that we shared.
He would want me to carry on being me and doing
all the things we enjoyed,
So that I can make stories we can share together
when we are reunited.

Today, Lord, I know that my brother is with you and
that you have ignited
An eternal light for him, which shines brightly in your
kingdom.
Help me to see his light as I journey on the road of
life.

Help me to feel his spirit as he walks alongside me.
Help me to hear his voice in the good days and the sad times that are ahead.
Take care of my brother, Lord. Look after him and keep him safe,
And try and keep him out of trouble,
Until we celebrate together in your glorious presence,
Amen.

57. A prayer for the loss of a parent

I suppose it is the way it is meant to be, Lord.
The natural order of life, some may say.
The parent should pass away and return to you
before the child does.
Yet that does not make the pain and the heartache
any easier.
Losing a connection to how I was created ...
Losing a friend who nurtured and cared for me for all
those years as I grew up,
Is difficult to process and put into words.
We had good times, Lord, times of happiness and
joy.
But sometimes our relationship was not easy.
Sometimes we argued and disagreed.
Sometimes, perhaps too often, we did not
communicate very well with each other And did not
express to each other what was in our hearts.
Maybe we never spoke the words to say how much
we loved each other.
But I know they loved me, even if they did not always
say the words.
And I love them, Lord, and miss them greatly.

There was never going to be a right moment for me
to say goodbye to my parent.
There will always be experiences that I want to share
with them.
There will always be conversations that I wish I had
taken the time
To have with them.
There will always be stories that they told me that I
wish I had written down,

So that I can refer back to them as a source of
comfort and as a guide
As I journey on the road of life.
Yet this will never happen now, and I feel sad at that
thought.

But there are the memories, Lord.
Memories that you have helped me to create.
Pictures that you have helped me to store up in the
album of my life.
Familiar words and phrases that will come back to
me when I least expect it,
To remind me that they live on in my heart and in my
soul.
As I say goodbye to my beloved parent for the final
time,
I shed more than just a few tears.
I shed tears of joy at the happy times we enjoyed
together.
I shed tears of sadness at the lost opportunities
And for the times when words were exchanged
which hurt and wounded us both.
I shed tears of gladness, for I know that a new life is
beginning for them
As they have been returned to your care.

As I say goodbye, Lord, I make a request of you,
One that I know you will grant for me.
Look after them and keep them safe.
I know, Lord, that you have ignited an eternal light for
them,
As they have been returned to your care,
A light that burns brightly in your kingdom.

May their light shine as a beacon of love and hope to guide and inspire me.
May my life reflect the best of what they wanted me to achieve,
So that when we are reunited together in your glorious presence,
We will have some amazing stories to tell each other,
Amen.

58. A prayer for the loss of a child

Why did you let this happen, Lord?
This is not the way life is meant to work.
The child should not pass away before the parent.
Why, Lord? Why?

I want to make sense of what has happened.
I want answers.
I want clarity and understanding.
I want the pain to go away.
I want this to end.
I want my child back in my arms so that I can cuddle
them
And tell them how much I love them.
Why did it have to end this way, and at such a
young, tender age?

They had their life ahead of them.
There were so many things I had planned for them.
There was so much we were going to do together.
There was so much I wanted them to achieve.
But all that has gone and I am left with pain and
heartache.
A part of my soul has gone with them.
There is a wound inside me, Lord. I don't know if it
will ever be healed.

I know, Lord, that my child is in your care and that
you will look after them.
You will tend to them, care for them, and love them.
Knowing you will be taking care of my child until we
are reunited together
Brings some comfort.

But I need to feel your presence in my life now more than ever.
I need to find the courage to move away from
This cycle of despair, anger, tears, and frustration.
I need to see your light, Lord. I need to know there is still hope in the world.

The journey I am on, Lord, will be long and it will be difficult.
There will not be a day that passes when I will not think about
The bundle of joy and happiness that I had in my life.
Help me to find a way out of this darkness,
And to bring some light and hope back into my life.
Help me to find the support I need,
Because I know I cannot make this journey on my own.
Give me the confidence, wisdom, and strength to make this journey.
Walk beside me, Lord, and be the tangible presence I need
To try and find something positive out of this awfulness.
Surround me with your love and hold on to me, Lord.
It is you, Lord, I depend on now more than ever,
And I place my trust in your unbreakable, eternal promises,
Amen.

59. A prayer for loss

A light has gone out

A light has gone out of my world, Lord,
A light I depended on, but it is not there anymore.
How do I cope, Lord?
What do I do?
We shared life together. We didn't do things apart.
And now I am alone.
And my heart is aching.
I have so many emotions in me,
I cry a lot. I am sad a lot.
I want to be on my own, but I am not sure that is
good for me.
I am just so confused, Lord.
Help me.
I know you are there for me.
Comfort me, Lord, in these dark days.
Help me to know your presence,
And to find the support I need.
Let me know what I should do,
And to have the courage to admit I need help and to
ask for help.
I pray this prayer in your name,
Amen.

60. A prayer for the loss of a friend

Lord, I have lost a friend, and my heart is hurting.
My heart feels so heavy when I think about them.

I feel my own grief and sadness at the loss of my
friend.
But I also feel grief and sadness for the family they
have left behind.
I really don't know what words I can say to you right
now.
I feel that a piece of my heart, and my soul, has
gone,
And I don't know if it will ever come back.

Although we were not in touch every day,
There was so much that we shared together.
There were so many adventures we had,
So much fun, so much laughter,
And on occasions maybe the odd prank or two.
Life wasn't always joy and happiness.
There were tears, Lord. Life is not always plain
sailing.
But whatever life threw at each of us,
We knew we would be able to talk
And, where we could, we would joke about the
situations we found ourselves in.

I have so many emotions in me,
Both for my friend and for me.
At times I want to cry a lot. At times I am sad.
But most of all, I just miss my friend
And I want to support the family they have left
behind.

In the dark days ahead, comfort our friend's family, Lord,
And those who loved and cared about my friend.
Help us to know your presence.
Help us to find the support we need.
Give us courage, Lord, and the strength to ask for help when we need it.
Be a light for us in this dark time.

And, Lord, help me to know your divine grace in this time of need.
Speak to me so that I may know what I can do to help.
Help me to find the words and actions
That can bring your love and peace into the lives of those who have been left behind.
Take good care of my friend, now that they have been returned to you.
Keep them safe,
So that one day we will be reunited together in your eternal glory,
With more stories and adventures to share together,
Amen.

61. A prayer for quiet reflection

Lord, I often come to you broken,
Often in pain, and with worries that I cannot let go.
With concerns about myself, my family, and my friends.
You, Lord, know what I am thinking.
You know what I need even before I ask you for help,
Because your grace and compassion transcend all human understanding.
And so, Lord, in a few moments of quiet,
I calm myself
And I reflect on the situations in my life that I need your help in.
And I lift these to you.

Lord, you are my rock, my salvation, my companion.
You are my source of hope and strength.
And most of all, Lord,
You are my friend.
In that sure and certain knowledge, Lord,
I commit this prayer and all my prayers
To your living, loving name,
Amen.

62. A prayer for today

Lord, give me confidence and courage today,
So that I can do the tasks I have to complete.
Keep me calm when things don't go according to
plan.
Give me the wisdom to know what I should do in
unexpected situations.
Help me to reflect the love you have for me
In all my words and in all the tasks I do this day and
always,
Amen.

63. A prayer for the homeless

Heavenly Father, too often I look at your world
Through the lens of my own perceptions.
I look at people, and I make instant judgements about
Why they are in the position that I find them, during that moment when I meet them.
I see people asking for money in the street, someone looking in the bin for food,
Or someone lying in a doorway at night, and it invokes a response in me.
Sometimes I respond with fear, sometimes I respond with disgust,
And sometimes I respond with pity and sympathy.

But you, Lord, would want me to respond
With empathy, kindness, and understanding.
When you walked on earth, Lord, all those years ago,
You never passed judgement on anyone because of their station in life.
You passed judgement on how people treated each other
And how they responded to others in their communities.
And you challenged me to love other people.
Just as you have, and always will, love me.

Lord, help me to challenge my beliefs and my perceptions.
Help me to see the world through your eyes,
To hear the world through your ears,
To feel the world through your compassionate heart.

I am called to be your servant.
I am called to do your work within this community.
So when I hear that call and feel that pull on my heart,
Help me to respond with courage and confidence to step out of my comfort zone
And step into the situations you are asking me to be in,
So that I can be a beacon of your light and hope,
Amen.

64. A prayer for night-time

I should be asleep

Lord, everything tells me I should be asleep and
resting,
But I find the hours when I should be sleeping
The most difficult.
My mind is clouded with thoughts that I cannot work
through.
I feel overwhelmed by the daily routine of my life,
And when everyone else goes to bed
The negative thoughts take over.
Calm me, Lord,
Help me to relax.
Help me to feel you close to me, Lord.
Help me to feel your reassurance and comfort.
Strengthen me, Lord, both physically and mentally.
Help me to remember you are always with me.
Help me to trust in you.
Help me to know your presence and feel your
soothing embrace.
Guide me this night, Lord, and all the days and
nights of my life,
Amen.

65. A prayer for night-time

I have had a difficult day

Lord, not everything today went according to plan.
But as I come to the end of the day
I give thanks for you being with me.
You know me, Lord, like no one else knows me.
You know my thoughts, my concerns, my joys, and
my sadness,
And you share in each one of these with me.
You are the quiet voice that speaks peace.
You are the calm reassurance I need.
When I feel overwhelmed and cannot find a calm
thought,
You are the soft pillow
I rest my weary head on at the end of the day.
You are the warm, protective blanket
That wraps around me
To help me feel safe and secure.
You are always there for me, Lord,
Watching over me and ready to listen to me.
Thank you, Lord, for being with me in everything I
have done.
Bless my rest time tonight and continue to be the
beacon of light in my life
That provides hope, comfort, and reassurance,
Amen.

66. A prayer for night-time

Help me to relax

Heavenly Father,
As the evening comes,
Help me to relax into your presence.
As I rest for a few moments,
Let my heart be calmed by your love,
Let my ears be open to your words, and
Let my eyes be open to your awesome wonders.
Grant, O gracious God, that I not only hear your word,
But understand it and receive it into my heart.
That I not only receive and understand your word,
But that I reveal it in my life
By living up to the calling that you have given to me.
Help me to show the love you have for me
Through my words and through the things that I do,
Amen.

67. A New Year's Eve prayer

It's New Year's Eve, Lord, and the final hours of this year are ebbing away.
I always approach New Year with a sense of anticipation and dread.
It is a time to begin again, a time to put the past behind me.
The previous twelve months are over, and this is a resetting of the clock.

But still, Lord, there is much of the last twelve months, and indeed the last few years,
That I will carry into the coming year.
My health is not as good as it once was.
I cannot call upon some of my friends and family as I have in the past.
People I have known for years are no longer around.
Some have moved on to pastures new.
Some are now in your loving care.

As I look back at the last twelve months,
I am reminded that I cannot stop the progress of time.
I cannot make the good times last longer, or the bad times end more quickly.
All I can do is to trust in you and to know you will be with me in all that I experience.

And as I reflect on the time that has passed,
I realise that you have been a constant presence
Throughout everything I have experienced.
You have guided me.
You have sent messages of hope and support to me.

You have surrounded me with people who care.

You have always reminded me that you are the same each day.
You accept me, even when I do things wrong.
You love me, even when my behaviour lets me down.
You forgive me, even when I feel that what I have done cannot be forgiven.
You accept me for who I am and what I am.

As I prepare to welcome in a new year, help me to focus on the positives.
To be thankful for what I have, and to make the most of
Each hour and each day that you have given to me.
Help me to accept the changes that will inevitably happen this year
With your grace and humility.
Help me to see my world through your eyes.
Help me to see the situations I find myself in as opportunities and not threats.
Help me to have the courage and the confidence to try new experiences.
Help me to expand the circle of my life and move out of my safe space.
So that together with you, Lord, I can grow and develop,
Both emotionally and spiritually.

But most of all, Lord, help me to continue to feel your presence by my side,
And to know that in all that I experience you will always be with me

As my companion, my guide, and my friend,
Amen.

68. A New Year prayer

Lord, thank you for being with me this year

Heavenly Father, as I reach the end of the year,
I give thanks for your presence in all my experiences
over the past twelve months.
I give thanks for all I have accomplished with your
help and guidance.
As I prepare myself for the time to come,
I recommit my life to you.
I rededicate myself to your glorious name,
And ask that you continue to be my light of hope and
inspiration.
I know, Lord, that there will be hard days and there
will be difficult times,
But I also know that with you by my side there will be
days of joy and laughter.
Whether the day be full of sunshine and light
Or tinged with darkness and difficulty,
I ask that you help me and let me know you are with
me.
Help me to feel your calm, soothing presence.
Help me to feel and show your love in this year to
come.
Give me strength, give me courage, give me
wisdom, give me grace,
Give me tolerance.
And help me to have a compassionate and
understanding heart,
So that I can reflect you in all the ways you have
asked me to serve,
Amen.

69. A New Year prayer

I rededicate my life to you, Lord

In the stillness of this place, Lord, I come, and I
worship you.
I lay aside my daily activities, and in prayer I
dedicate my life to you.
When you came to live among us, you came to be
my guide
To teach me, to lead me, to show me how I should
be with other people.
You explained in clear and simple words and actions
How I should behave, how I should forgive, and how
I should love.
As I journey into a new year,
Let the love you have placed in my heart burn for
you
And radiate from me into the world.
Help me to carry some of the burdens of this world
through my prayers,
So that I can bring comfort and hope into the dark
places
That so badly need the Christ light I celebrate,
Which comes into this world each Christmastime,
Amen.

70. A New Year prayer

Help me to proclaim your glory

As I journey into a new year and a new decade,
Enrich me with your grace and empower me with
your spirit
So that I will be the messenger you have called me
to be,
Proclaiming your word and telling your story
In the sure and certain knowledge that
You will never leave me and will return to me in
glory,
Amen.

Christian Festivals

1. An Advent prayer

Heavenly Father, the time of Advent has arrived.
A time of joy, of hope, of reflection.

Advent invokes all these emotions in me, Lord.
Each week I see a candle being lit,
And it reminds me of the gift that was given to the
world.
I hear the familiar stories about your coming,
And I am reminded of the sacrifices that were made.
I am reminded of the faith that Mary and Joseph had
in each other and in you,
And the love they had for you and for each other.

Following you, Lord, is never easy,
And Advent should be a time when I remember
much more than just your birth.
I should remember what your birth meant to the
world.
I should remember what was being given to me:
The light of the world, which can help me in all the
days of my life.

But all too often that message is lost, Lord.
In this season so full of music, lights, tinsel, wrapping
paper, presents, and food,
I can easily forget the real reason Christmas is
celebrated.
The real gift that you gave.
A gift that means so much to me.

Your coming, Lord, brought into my world a light of hope.
A light that has brought to me joy, happiness, and thanksgiving.
A light that brought me understanding, reassurance, and, above all, forgiveness.
Through you, Lord, I am forgiven. I am born again in your name.

As I begin the journey of the season of Advent
Help me to feel the hope and the knowledge
That I am loved by you.
Help me to remember that anything is possible with you.
Help me to remember that the gift you gave me
Is the gift that provides me with everlasting faith, hope, strength,
And encouragement.
Help me to show how much your presence in my world has meant to me.
Help me to bring the hope of this season
To all the people around me.
Let my words and actions reflect the love I have for you
And the love you have for me,
This day and always,
Amen.

2. An Advent prayer

Beginning the journey

Heavenly Father, as I begin the journey of the
season of Advent
I pray my faith in you is refreshed,
My love for you is emboldened,
And the light you placed in my heart,
The day I decided to follow you, shines brighter.
Help me to see beyond the trappings of tinsel,
presents, and food
To the real gift that was given, more than two
thousand years ago.
Help me to remember that the gift you gave me,
The light of the world that shines in all situations,
Is the gift that provides me with everlasting faith,
hope, strength,
And encouragement.
Help me, Lord, when I am challenged by your call
To respond to your first request
And not hide from you
And avoid what it is you ask me to do,
Amen.

3. A prayer for journeying through Advent

Lord, the time of Advent is here.
A time of joy, a time of excitement, a time of hope, a time of opportunity,
And a time to reflect.
Your coming, Lord, gave me the light that is the centre of my world,
A light that is the hope and the salvation of all.

As I prepare myself for the days and weeks that are before me,
Help me to not get carried away by the rush and haste
That so often come at this time of year.
Help me to stop, to listen, to watch, to learn, to calm myself both inside and out.
Help me to look for you in all I see and do.
Help me to hear your voice in the carols and the music.
Help me to feel your presence in the good times and the sad times.

As I travel through this Advent season
Help me to celebrate and give thanks for the precious gift
That your coming gave to me,
And to a world that is in so much need of hope and love,
Amen.

4. A prayer for others in the season of Advent

I know, Lord, that in this season of Advent
There will be individuals who are dreading the
thought of Christmas.
There will be people who will not have enough to eat
While others will buy so much food that it will be
thrown away and go to waste.
There will be people who will not receive any
presents,
While others will have so many presents
That they forget which person bought them which
present.
There will be people who don't have a home where
they can hang up their stocking,
Who sleep outside in the cold and wet,
While others turn up the central heating and throw off
the duvet.
There will be people who don't have access to
medicines or hospitals,
While others send for medical help without good
reason.
There will be people for who Christmas is no
different from any other day,
And who will continue to feel the pain of loneliness,
isolation, fear, and anxiety.

In this season of Advent,
Teach me not only to pray for those who will go
without this Christmas,
But to respond to their need by giving generously
from my own means
In any way that I can.
Help me to remember that the gift you gave me,

The light of the world that shines in all situations, is the gift that provides me
With everlasting faith, hope, strength, and encouragement.
Help me, Lord, when I am challenged by your call
To respond on the first tug of my heart and my mind,
And to not avoid or dismiss you.
Help me not to hide from what it is you are asking me to do
And to be the beacon of light you have called me to be,
Amen.

5. A Christmas prayer

Lord, you are so often overlooked and ignored.
You were rejected by so many when you came to
live among us,
Even though you are the most important person to
have walked on this earth.
You were seen as unimportant,
Another prophet to be listened to and exalted for a
while,
But then discounted, insulted, abused, and then
crucified.

And yet, Lord, your presence is so needed in the
lives of so many.
Your coming, Lord, is longed for,
Even by those who do not really know who or what
you are.
It is searched for even by those who do not know
what they are seeking.
It is prayed for by those who know of your grace,
power, love, and majesty.
It is called for in the silent screams of those who
need help.
It is asked for by those who know there is something
missing in their lives.

As the time of Advent ends and the time of
Christmas begins,
I ask that you make yourself a tangible and visible
presence to all who are in need.
I ask that you awaken the bodies, minds, and souls
Of all who seek forgiveness and acceptance.

I ask that your powerful healing love enters the hearts of all who are praying, calling, and asking for help.

I ask that you enter my life
And open my eyes, my ears, and my heart to the world around me.
Inspire me and help me to know how I can make a difference.
Give me the courage and the confidence to do the tasks you ask me to undertake.
Help me to be more like the babe of Christmas:
Welcoming strangers, nurturing loved ones,
constantly growing and evolving
Into the person you want me to be,
This day and always,
Amen.

6. A prayer for Christmas Day

Lord, the day is finally here
And I welcome you with love in my heart.
As I prepare myself for the day ahead,
I ask that you be with me.

Christmas Day holds so many memories.
I remember the times growing up,
And what Christmas meant to me as a child.
I remember the traditions, the gifts, the music, and
the food.
Sometimes we had a lot to celebrate,
And we had lots of presents and food to eat.
Sometimes life was difficult,
And there wasn't much food or many presents.
But always, Lord, I had you to give thanks for.
Each memory I have, Lord, I treasure,
For they helped me grow into the person I am today.

Christmas often gives me a feeling of hope and love.
It is a time for my family and friends.
In the noise and haste of this day,
Help me to pause and reflect.
Help me to remember the good times with joy.
When I reflect on the sad times, give me strength
and comfort.
Help me to remember that in all times of my life you
are with me.

Lord, be with my family and with me.
Help me to keep the Christmases of the past, the
present, and the future in my heart.

Stay close to me, Lord, so that I may constantly know your love and peace,
As I rejoice at the light of the world being at the centre of my life,
Amen.

7. A Christmas prayer

It's a sad time for me, Lord

Lord, Christmas for me feels a sad and lonely time.
It is a day no different to the other days that have
gone before.
I am told I should feel joy and happiness,
But I don't feel that way.
I feel lonely and isolated.
My life feels like a dark place, full of fear.

Help me to ask, find, and have the courage to accept
help.
Help me to have the inner strength and confidence
To step out into the unknown.
Let me feel your calmness when things get a little
fraught.
Help me to know your calm, soothing love in the
quiet times,
And to feel your arms comforting me when I
remember Christmases past,
Amen,

8. A Christmas prayer

Help me to focus on you, Lord

Heavenly Father, help me in this season of
Christmas
To keep you at the centre of everything I do.
May your light that I celebrate coming into the world
each Christmas
Always be with me.
Let me always know your presence in everything I
do.
And may I always remember that I am yours, Lord,
And you are mine forever and ever,
Amen.

9. A prayer for Pentecost

Thank you for this day, Lord,
Thank you for sending your Holy Spirit just as you
promised you would.
The day of Pentecost was the day when you sent the
Holy Spirit
Into the lives of your followers.
It was the day when the fire of the Holy Spirit brought
your word
To a global audience.
Everyone who heard your message
Was able to proclaim their love for you
In all the languages of the world.

Lord, the gift of your Holy Spirit
Can provide so much strength and power in my life.
But all too often, Lord, I don't let your fire into my
heart.
All too often I try and do things on my own.
I try to be my own strength and source of power.
And that does not always work out well.

I want to have that unwavering trust that the disciples
had in you.
I want to know the fire of your presence in my life
each day.
I want to trust in you and have the confidence to
speak of what you mean to me.
When I am afraid,
I need your Holy Spirit to provide comfort to me.
At times when I am unsure of what to do,
I need your Holy Spirit to provide me with
reassurance.

When I am weak and feel I cannot go on,
I need your Holy Spirit to provide me with strength.
When I cannot find the words to express what I want to say,
I need your Holy Spirit to give me the words I can speak so that I can be heard.

Lord, I need your Holy Spirit as my helper and my guide.
I need your spirit in me to help me to be more like you.
Help me to be more open to your love.
Help me to be more acceptant of your holy fire in my life.
Help me to carry the gift of the Holy Spirit in my heart,
And to trust and rely on its power and strength,
In all the situations of my life,
Amen.

10. A prayer for harvest

Lord, harvest is a time for me to celebrate the
wonders of your world.
It is a time to be thankful for the wind, for the rain,
and for the sunshine.
A time to be grateful for the animals of the world,
Whether they are on the land, in the sea, or in the
sky.
I thank you for the food that I can eat.
I thank you for the water that is widely available.
I thank you for the love and commitment of the
farmers and growers.
I thank you for the amazing gifts you have given to
me.

But when I stop and think, Lord,
There is so much of what I have that I take for
granted.
I take for granted there will be water when I turn on
the tap.
I take for granted I can buy fresh fruit, vegetables,
and meat.
I take for granted that the trees will blossom in
spring, fill out in summer,
Change colour in autumn, and rest in winter.
I take for granted that there will be fish in the ocean,
Birds in the sky, and animals in the field.
I take for granted there will be wind, rain, and
sunshine,
And that each of these will be provided in equal
measure.

And yet, Lord, that is not how the world works.
There are parts of the world that have no rain, and crops fail.
There places in the world where there are food shortages
And people are starving.
There are places in the world where fresh meat, fruit, and vegetables
Are not available.
There are places in your world where families cannot afford a simple meal.
And these families live in prosperous countries.

I want to remember the people who are less fortunate than me.
I ask you, Lord, to inspire me to do more to help the people around me in need.
I ask you, Lord, to challenge my perception and take me out of my comfort zone.
Help me think of ways I can help others.

I may not have much to offer myself,
I may not be able to make a grand gesture of money or food,
But I can share the gifts and the talents you have given me.
I can spend a few minutes each day in prayer and reflection.
I can ask you to help me not to take for granted all that I have
And to always be thankful for you and all that you have given me.

Help me, Lord, this harvest time,
To look beyond the hymns and the decorations in the church,
And to think of what more I can do
To show the love I have for your world
And the people less fortunate than me,
Amen.

11. A church anniversary prayer

Lord, on this anniversary day I give thanks
For all the memories this church has given me.
I give thanks
For all the special moments I have shared in this
place.
I give thanks
For all the people I have met, and for all they have
done to help me.
Looking back, Lord, brings joy and tears mixed
together.
Each memory, each moment, each person,
Has helped to mould, develop, and educate me into
the person I am today.
I want to hold on to the past,
To never let go of what I knew and loved.
But time does not stand still,
And change will always happen.

So, on this day,
I ask that you be with me.
Help me to keep in my heart
The special times I have enjoyed in this place.
Help me to keep in my mind
The memories of the experiences I enjoyed.
And help me to always remember
That in every moment, both good and bad,
You were there with me,
And you will always be with me.
Because, as Scripture says,
You are the same, Lord, yesterday, today, and
forever.

And for that, on this day and every day,
I give you thanks and praise,
Amen.

Printed in Great Britain
by Amazon